UNDEAD

REVIVED RESUSCITATED REBORN

UNDEAD

CLAY MORGAN

Abingdon Press
NASHVILLE

UNDEAD
REVIVED, RESUSCITATED, REBORN

Copyright © 2012 Clay Morgan

This book is printed on acid-free paper.

Library of Congress Cataloging-in-Publication Data has been requested.

ISBN: 978-1-4267-5345-9

All scripture quotations, unless otherwise indicated, are taken from the Holy Bible, New International Version®, NIV®. Copyright © 1973, 1978, 1984, 2011 by Biblica, Inc.™ Used by permission of Zondervan. All rights reserved worldwide. www.zondervan.com. The "NIV" and "New International Version" are trademarks registered in the United States Patent and Trademark Office by Biblica, Inc.™

Scripture quotations from *THE MESSAGE*. Copyright © by Eugene H. Peterson 1993, 1994, 1995, 1996, 2000, 2001, 2002. Used by permission of NavPress Publishing Group.

Scripture quotations taken from the New American Standard Bible®, Copyright © 1960, 1962, 1963, 1968, 1971, 1972, 1973, 1975, 1977, 1995 by The Lockman Foundation. Used by permission. (www.Lockman.org)

Scripture quotations marked NLT are taken from the *Holy Bible,* New Living Translation, copyright © 1996, 2004, 2007. Used by permission of Tyndale House Publishers, Inc., Carol Stream, Illinois 60188. All rights reserved.

12 13 14 15 16 17 18 19 20 21—10 9 8 7 6 5 4 3 2 1
MANUFACTURED IN THE UNITED STATES OF AMERICA

To Mom and Aunt, the greatest people to ever show me how to come back from the dead. I love you dearly.

CONTENTS

INTRODUCTION

The first time I realized that people die I was four, and my great-grandmother was dying on a studio couch in our dining room. She had been born in the nineteenth century and was eighty-nine years old, an impossible age to a little boy.

I was sick too, though not with the serious kind of sickness that happens to old people. I awoke from a terrible dream that night after taking bitter medicine and falling asleep upstairs. Miserable and afraid, I went downstairs, walked past the deathbed scene, and threw up all over the yellow kitchen wall. That little contribution of mine probably wasn't too helpful to the family.

I couldn't see past the backs of family members huddled around that couch. I don't think I was supposed to see. The whole scene seemed forbidden somehow. I wanted to look but I also didn't want to. That's the way it is with death, I learned. Most of us spend our lives trying not to think about it while at the same time being irresistibly pulled toward it.

Some people have told me they clearly remember the first time *they* realized they were going to die. For me, it seems like something I always knew. I grew up in a family of realists who taught me early on that death is a part of life. Losing my great gram and grandma before my fifth birthday was a part of that lesson. Then there's the time they accidentally left me at the funeral home with a bunch of strangers and a corpse, but we'll get to that a bit later.[1]

Dying didn't pack too much of a punch for me back then. I wasn't even fully grown let alone old, and I'd been taught that I'd go to heaven, which sounded pretty nice (even though my tiny mind was having trouble with the concept of eternity). I had other things to worry about such as math and getting stung by bees every time my mom dressed me in bright pollenlike colors on hot summer days.

Death is everywhere when you grow up the way I did in the conservative Christian church world of the 1980s and 1990s. You constantly hear how Jesus died or you are going to die or *somebody* is going to die before church or youth group ends. And if we all make it out of church alive then someone might just die on their way home, so we better think about that and get ready. Such were the lessons of my religious upbringing. Not exactly the happiest delivery for a message of hope.

Death isn't the end of existence, some say, but what if death isn't the end of life? What if there could be life beyond the grave, a physical existence that defies mortality? What if there isn't just death and life, but death and *undeath*?

---

1. My therapist should be here by then. Kidding. It's chapter 3.

There's actually a few millennia worth of stories that explore this idea—from ancient legends to biblical records to modern movies. And these stories thrill us. We are fascinated by tales of the living dead because as much as we try to block out the scary reality of death we can't quite stop staring at it and pondering the possibilities beyond this life. In fact, stories of the undead generate billions of dollars these days. I guess we've figured that if we're going to contemplate our own mortality we might as well get some popcorn and cool special effects.

THE MUPPET UNDEAD AND FRIENDS

For many of us, our first undead experience was with a vampire named Count von Count. I don't remember being afraid of the Count, but he did live in a spooky, cobweb-infested castle on Sesame Street. Lightning flashed and thunder crashed every time he counted stuff. Maybe this explains my lifelong aversion to math.

And then Count Chocula is a close second. Who knew vampires really craved chocolate cereal? In hindsight, it's kind of funny that my caring parents plopped me down in front of cute and lovable fanged killers every morning. Truth told those guys were about as scary as the modern batch of dysfunctional *Twilight* vamps. So maybe we're just getting back to our Sesame Street roots these days, but one thing I know: Real vampires don't sparkle.[2] But perhaps

---

2. My apologies if I've offended Team Edward. For the record, when it comes to pale, mournful movie characters named Edward I'm a Scissorhands man.

the first *real* vampires for me were *The Lost Boys*. None of them sparkled or went to high school. They ate people and terrified us. I remember being afraid to go the beach for years after watching that film.[3] That movie also highlighted the rules of occult mythology. Turns out if you invite a vampire into your home then traditional defenses such as crosses, holy water, and garlic become ineffective. I made it a point never technically to invite people I really didn't know into my house after that. My sister's boyfriends were under constant suspicion.

Vampires weren't the only living-dead creatures I had to deal with—next came the zombies, the first being Michael Jackson. In "Thriller," it looks like any other Saturday night when MJ puts on his red jacket and takes his girl to the movies, except that once the music starts playing he turns into a zombie.[4] That video was a real turning point for him, I think, because he seemed to get scarier and scarier after that.

The fictional undead creatures multiply from there, especially when it comes to movies. You either like scary movies or you don't, and for whatever reason, I've always enjoyed stories that are designed to frighten. A film like *28 Days Later* delivers suspense by showing a world gone wrong where millions of people fall victim to a deadly virus. The horrifying transformation from the time a person is infected until the time they become an undead threat is often only seconds. Good storytellers leave me white-knuckled and holding my breath, and I love it.

---

3. My beanpole physique didn't help either, so I maintained the pale complexion of a vampire for years while lacking their strength. Or any strength.

4. A dancing zombie, admittedly with some pretty sweet moves.

Writers and directors of supernatural thrillers play around with the mythological canon from time to time. For example, Marvel created a vampire protagonist called Blade who can survive in daylight like Bram Stoker's original Dracula. (Most other vampires these days burst into flames if sunlight hits them.) Zombies are different too; sometimes they develop cognitive abilities along the way as if they are evolving. Director and zombie godfather George Romero is known for this type of development.

THE D WORD

Part of the appeal of these stories is the ability to challenge the status quo. It's satisfying to manipulate reality through fiction because real life doesn't offer too many unexpected miracles. We die from the same types of things over and over: heart problems, cancer, accidents, one another. When it's our time to go we can no more expect to cheat death than we can expect to be reanimated by the bite of a viral creature. There's just death. That's the way it is.

Sometimes the best we can do in response to the certainty of death is to laugh, most likely a nervous reaction. That's how we end up with comedies like *Zombieland* and *Shaun of the Dead*, stories that borrow once-fierce creatures from the horror genre in order to play up the absurdities of life and death. You might not think an apocalypse is that funny, but if we're all doomed without hope and there's no point to existence then laughing about it makes as much sense as any other reaction.

Of course many of us believe that there is hope of existence after death. But that doesn't mean I'm comfortable with our mortal situation or anywhere close to being free from despair. My fear of monsters may have disappeared a long time ago, but the anxiety over death has never left me. I'm not alone.

After all, most of us are kind of obsessed with death. That's the way it's always been for humanity.

People have always sought ways to find life beyond the grave. Life spans were much shorter in recent centuries, so men and women of old had even fewer years to contemplate their fate. You can see this preoccupation by studying most any culture. Ancient Hebrew writers, for example, used many metaphors to describe the brevity of life, describing our days on this planet as a vapor, a breath, a mist, a shadow, a grass that withers and dies, a box of chocolates.[5] Death is like a zombie: not as scary when you're looking at it from a distance but terrifying when it's pounding on your door. Close equals scary.

We only get so much time on earth, so even though we're talking about the undead, understand that this book is about living. I think we just have to talk about the reality of death in order for the gift of life to make sense.

I've always been fascinated by stories of people coming back to life. That type of thing has a wow factor that's kind of hard to top. Most of these stories are fictional, but a few actually come down to us through the historical record—such claims always make

---

5. Oh wait. I think that last one was Forrest Gump.

my historian's heart beat faster.[6] Some of these stories are designed to be terrifying whereas others are beautiful and still a few more are just funny, but all of these tales are used to filter views on the meaning of life, death, and God. I don't know many people who can think about any one of those three things for long without raising new questions and coming to new conclusions only to circle back and start all over again.

There are good reasons for our cultural fascination with people who can't be stopped by death, and I'm not just talking about the cool special effects. If you're up for this little literary journey you might be surprised at what those factors are. In fact, I hope it might just change the way you see life and death.

---

6. I don't mean that I keep a dead historian's heart on my desk. I teach history and political science at a couple of different colleges in Pittsburgh.

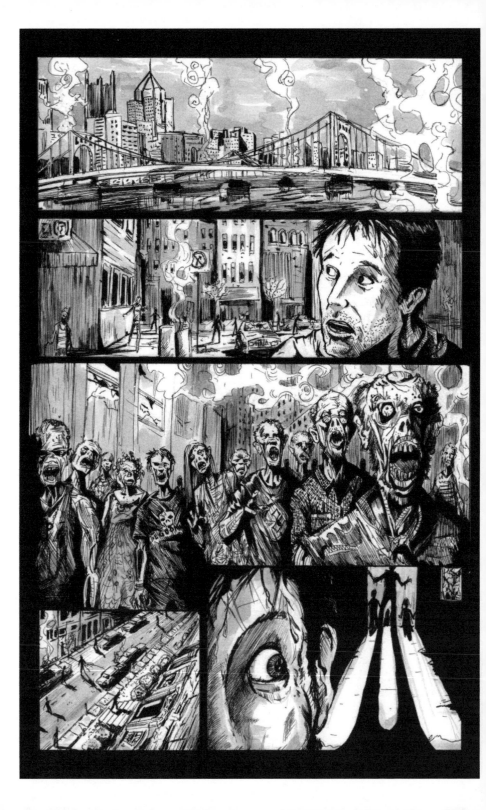

CHAPTER 1

THE LIVING DEAD

Death is a very dull, dreary affair, and my advice
to you is to have nothing whatsoever to do with it.
—W. Somerset Maugham

After teaching a class at the University of Pittsburgh one crisp, autumn day I walked around a corner and was attacked by a zombie. It's probably not what you think; there was no biting, moaning, or hacking. The zombie just mistook me for a human.

Humans vs. Zombies (HvZ) is a game of moderated tag being played by tens of thousands of people, particularly college students, all over the world. Games involve strategy and teamwork and take a few days to complete. Bandanas indicate participation—on the arm for a human, on the head or neck for a zombie.

1

Since the creation of HvZ in 2005, the phenomenon has grown so much that student clubs and organizations dedicated to it already exist on campuses around the globe.

Pittsburgh is a fitting setting for zombie mayhem, since, after all, the modern popularity of the living dead can be traced to George Romero's cult classic movie *Night of the Living Dead*, filmed in the 'Burgh in 1968. With that film, Romero revolutionized an entire genre and converted zombies from the more traditional witch-doctor victims they had long been into flesh-eating hunters. Eventually, human brains became the entrée of choice for these monsters, and more than forty years later, the undead continue to draw in viewers and consumers by the millions.

Books, movies, and video games drive zombie zeal in the twenty-first century. We just can't get enough of them these days. Thanks to the internet, a massive zombie subculture exists across a variety of websites and social media networks. There are even plans for a zombie musical as Broadway producers have already secured the rights to Michael Jackson's "Thriller". The American government even got in on the hype in May 2011 when the Centers for Disease Control released a Zombie Apocalypse preparation guide as a clever gimmick to raise awareness for appropriate responses to natural disasters. Reaction to the humorous ploy was so overwhelming that the website crashed for a few hours.[1]

Like the creatures at the heart of this phenomenon, the popularity of undead creatures doesn't seem to be dying anytime soon.

---

1. The CDC didn't stop there either. They've since turned their clever take on emergency preparedness into a zombie novella. You can check it out at www.cdc.gov/phpr/zombies_novella.htm.

Well, technically zombies are already dead, but that's the problem. You can whack off their arms or put one in their chest and they'll just keep marching toward you like they were strolling down the aisle in a grocery store.

We are compelled by beings that can't be stopped by death. This attraction makes a bit more sense with something like vampires, who are increasingly portrayed as romantic, beautiful, and heroic. That's quite a different thing than zombies, which represent only decay and death and are considered to be completely beyond redemption. On the surface, the popularity of horrible creatures that are frightening, gruesome, and evil doesn't make much sense. Yet the undead generate billions of dollars in revenue worldwide.

ZOMBIES IN THE MIRROR

What do we see in a zombie that's so compelling? The short and perhaps surprising answer is that we see ourselves. Zombies were people once. They were humans who ate Skittles and had babies and danced badly at weddings. They drank coffee, shopped for bedding, downloaded music, blew out birthday candles, and attended church. This familiarity is seen in the way they're dressed: frightening ghouls wearing bathrobes and name tags and Dockers. When we see them ambling down the street, we fear them and imagine how close we are to becoming them at the same time. Other monsters are different since we usually don't under-

3

stand where they came from or what they even are, but we know exactly what zombies are: regular people who didn't stay dead. Ultimately, we project ourselves onto monsters because it helps make sense out of our human nature.

We also see one another in zombies. Relationships drive zombie stories, and they are filled with friends, siblings, spouses, and parents who can transition from loved ones to enemies in seconds. We're compelled by the idea of a loved one becoming a deadly enemy so quickly. In *28 Days Later,* one of my favorites, a likable character named Frank is accidentally infected by the "rage" virus, which takes effect very quickly. Frank realizes instantly that he's been infected and has only seconds to tell his teenage daughter, Hannah, that he loves her while trying to stagger away and not hurt anyone. In an instant he goes from protector to threat, and his friend Jim is suddenly faced with the terrifying task of doing whatever must be done to stop one of the few people left in the world to care about. It's not just imagining what we would do if grandma or hubby suddenly became a flesh-eating monster. It's about betrayal, a piercing emotional hit by someone we trust.

We also see zombies in us. We're self-centered in that we only get one narrow perspective through which to process reality. Call us self-focused if that erases the sting a bit. We simply look at ourselves more than anyone else. We want to like what we see, but that's usually not the case, so we present versions of ourselves that will appeal to the rest of the world. Those public masks may fool the people around us, but it's a different story when we look in the mirror. Truth always claws its way out of our hearts. Those dark parts of who we can be when we're at our worst can repulse us like decay-riddled zombies. Zombies represent complete depravity, pure evil, the worst a person can become. They offer nothing but death. They have no hope. We cheer for their destruction because conquering evil is good. And when we applaud the end of such evil, a part of us feels vindicated as though the darkest parts of us can be overcome.

But we also see other things in these fearsome creatures. One of their most striking features is that they, in a sense, conquer the grave. At the very least, death does not stop them. If we fear death, then what do we make of someone who can't be stopped by it? Any being with that kind of power gets our attention.

Ironically, living-dead beings like zombies are a cultural phenomenon because they reflect something that's true about people, both who we think we are and who we actually are. Observing them opens a window into how we think about mortality, eternity, and life as we know it, and that's what this book aims to do: explore issues of life, death, and life after death.

THE UNDEAD ARE DAMNED

I'm guessing that most of us today don't contemplate the possibility of eternal damnation each morning while sipping on coffee and munching on cereal. I mean, on Mondays maybe, but *every* day is just overdoing it. It's hard for us in the twenty-first century to understand what a preoccupation that concept was for most people in earlier centuries. As I study and teach the first few thousand years of Western civilization I'm struck by how focused those societies were on securing eternal salvation. Ancient Sumerians, Egyptians, Hebrews, and many others lived in a dangerous time of short life spans. Most of them expected to face eternity sooner rather than later. And they believed in an eternal existence.

In the seventeenth century, William Penn—the man who founded my home state of Pennsylvania—casually described the natural mind-set of his contemporaries when he said, "Death is no more than a turning of us over from time to eternity."[2] The logic of ancients followed pretty simply from such a foundation. Life is short and then you die. After that, some sort of an accounting would be necessary. History is filled with the creation of one religion after another as people attempted to work out a system for securing a win at the end judgment.

Conversely, these days we spend most of our time thinking about how to prolong our time on earth, because we can—at least we think we can. Through the science of vitamins, gyms, plastic surgery clinics, and more, we are hoping to manufacture the Fountain of Youth. But the simple idea of having food every day and free time would have blown the minds of ancient folks.

Yet despite our modern luxury of distraction, apprehension over the hereafter is still woven into our DNA. Postapocalyptic stories such as zombie movies force us to think about such things.

---

2. William Penn, *Fruits of Solitude,* vol. 1, part 3. The Harvard Classics (New York: P. F. Collier & Son, 1909–14); Bartleby.com, 2001. www.bartleby.com/1/3/.

We have to admire how themes of life and death, eternity and damnation are bottled up in the dialogue of these tales. The characters who grapple with such issues never get squeaky-clean resolution because reality doesn't work that way. Life is frustratingly gray, although we're often preoccupied by simplistic notions of black and white, right and wrong. So if life is this confusing, how much more lost are we when it comes to death? There's a reason the afterlife is often called the great unknown.

One of the interesting ways we can measure this human fear is by looking at folklore from around the world over the centuries. Every society tells stories of monsters; vampires, for example, appear in some form in legends from many different cultures. Modern vampires of the cinema make us forget some of what made those creatures so frightening to previous generations. They were damned souls—that's why religious items such as crosses and holy water were used to combat them. The biggest fear was not simply that they had sharp teeth and fast feet but also that they were *soul takers*. To be bitten and turned was to be lost forever, condemned to the dark side for all eternity.

We can't understand how terrifying that prospect was to highly religious societies of centuries past, when a higher percentage of people believed in the existence of a soul and an eternal destination for that soul than is typical today. This children's prayer from more than three hundred years ago shows us a little about the mentality of past centuries:

Now I lay me down to sleep,

I pray the Lord my soul to keep,

If I shall die before I wake,

I pray the Lord my soul to take.[3]

That doesn't sound like a typical bedtime thought for our kids today, at least not one I would teach my kids. Modern vampires have been holy-watered down, becoming soap opera characters with gelled hair and pouty expressions who feel like no one understands them. The transformation in how we view such monsters has something to do with a culturally diminished focus on eternity; if eternal damnation doesn't matter to us as much these days, then vamps lose some sizzle in the theological impact department. This cultural shift from sizzle to sparkle provides a clue about our current level of focus on eternal things.

The undead can also get our attention by making us think about our soul, whether or not it exists, and what that reality means to each one of us. We are moved by the idea of a creature without hope of redemption. We are compelled by the hopelessness of the soul. Can there be any redemption for a vampire or zombie? It's hard to imagine any redemption for the undead. There is a totality to the nature of these beings; they are all-consuming, solely focused, and completely beyond salvation. So as thoughts of redemption cycle through our minds we can't help relating to the questions in a personal way: What about *my* soul?

---

3. The most famous place this prayer appeared was in *The New England Primer*, the most well-known schoolbook in America before the Revolution.

THE UNDEAD REPRESENT THE END OF THE WORLD

One of the reasons that zombies intrigue us in a different way than some other creatures is because they tend to represent the apocalypse. They aren't exactly introverts, after all, but prefer to get out and mingle and welcome new friends into the fold. Bites become the new handshake. It's more effective than Facebook, really. As a result, the population of those who still prefer Twinkies to brains dwindles rapidly. *World War Z* author Max Brooks says that, "Other monsters may threaten individual humans, but the living dead threaten the entire human race. . . . Zombies are slate wipers."[4]

My Great Aunt Mitzie used to always say that the world is going to hell in a handbasket.[5] I still have no idea what that means, but I do know we are obsessed with the end of the world. We've long had apocalypse on the brain.[6] The year 2012 just happens to be the latest date of ultimate doom because centuries ago the Mayan people created a calendar that ends in 2012. We've taken that limit as a sign that the world will end in the twenty-first century, just as the ancients predicted. John Cusack even made a movie about it. Maybe the Mayans knew something about the ultimate end of human existence, but I'm thinking some guy's hand

---

4. Craig Wilson, "Zombies Lurch into Popular Culture via Books, Plays, More," *USA Today*. www.usatoday.com/life/books/news/2009-04-08-zombies-pop-culture_N.htm.

5. I don't recommend traveling anywhere in a handbasket unless you're E.T.

6. The funny and intelligent Jason Boyett wrote a good book on this called *Pocket Guide to 2012* in which he sums up most of these foolish predictions.

just got tired and he stopped chiseling. In the summer of 2011 a man named Harold Camping attracted a lot of attention by declaring that the rapture would take place on May 21, 2011, at exactly something o'clock, give or take daylight savings time and a boatload of delusion.

Well, we're still here.

You're really taking a risk by predicting when the world is going to end. It's a much smarter play to predict that the world *isn't* going to end anytime soon at all. That's what I'm going with. Because if I'm wrong, well, no one will be left to say anything about it.

It's fascinating that we can believe anyone who claims to know with absolute certainty when the world will end. Many of these doomsday prophets have attracted followers who believe that the Bible is an important book, but apparently none of them care for the verses of the Bible that say that no one knows when the world will end (Mark 13:32, for example). I've even heard people combine biblical prophecies and science by claiming that God may use a zombie virus plague to end the world.

Though we've been anticipating the end of the world for centuries, lately we've made it a little more interesting by adding zombies and Twitter. *The Walking Dead* is an intense TV show about zombies and the end of the world. In one episode a character named Dr. Edwin Jenner says of the zombie apocalypse, "This is our extinction event."[7] To many of us, a zombie apocalypse makes as much sense as anything else to wipe out humankind.

---

7. This scene appears in the last episode of season 1 called "TS-19."

Zombies have always been apocalyptic figures. We're drawn to these stories even more when the world seems to be falling apart. The first film in the genre was called *White Zombie* and came out in 1932, right as the Great Depression was reaching its peak. Another four zombie movies were released over the next decade while the world struggled against economic devastation and the fascist threat of world domination led by the evil regime of Adolf Hitler. Interestingly, zombie films receded through the 1950s, a much more peaceful era of postwar prosperity, particularly in America.

It's also not a coincidence that the movie that basically created the modern zombie canon came out in 1968, one of the darkest years in modern history. George Romero's *Night of the Living Dead* resonated with audiences that year—one of the worst years America had ever experienced. Tragedies struck in quick succession in 1968: the Vietnam War had already divided the country by January of that year when the Tet Offensive showed anxious citizens that the end of the conflict was not coming soon. Then both Martin Luther King Jr., and Senator Robert Kennedy were assassinated within two months of each other. Racial divisions and protests drove national conflict as many found ways to escape the madness of it all. By that point, flesh-eating zombies fit in quite well with the absurdity of life that millions of people found so hard to understand.

Tragedy and zombie popularity are inversely proportional. The worse things get, the more we buy into the apocalypse. The 1980s and 1990s weren't perfect but were relatively peaceful and prosperous. Not surprising then that you won't find massive main-stream appeal to zombies like we see in a post–9/11 world. Even ZomComs or zombedies (zombie comedies) like *Shaun of the Dead* rake in millions these days. If the economy's in the tank and the world's about to end, many people figure we might as well find some way to laugh about the demise of everything.

THE UNDEAD ARE UNCOMPROMISING

Some of the greatest people in history have been bravely uncompromising. Individuals such as Martin Luther King Jr., Gandhi, and Abraham Lincoln lived admirable lives by refusing to flinch as they stood against immoral practices of their day. It's great to watch men and women stand up for what's right without wavering. These are the kind of people we want to get behind and follow.

On the flipside, though, are those people who are equally unwavering in their push to bring evil on others. When it comes to zombies, they just keep coming. No matter how many you kill, they don't stop. They won't recognize you. No reason can persuade them. They don't discriminate as they prey on living things. They are amoral—right and wrong hold no influence over the constant drive of insatiable hunger. You either escape or kill them. Unlike the living, their existence doesn't get blurred in the gray areas.

Chris Weed—one of the guys who created *Humans vs. Zombies*—says that zombies "represent the inevitability of death.

You can shoot one or two but eventually you're gonna die. And you have to come to terms with that. You can run from death as long as you want, but it's gonna get you eventually."[8]

Zombies are driven by uncompromising cravings. Most of us can relate to the dangers of an appetite gone wild. I'm not just talking about food; we all tend to go after something—a job, a drug, or another person, for example—with reckless abandon at some point during our lives. One of the dangers of living in a world chock full of options and freedom is that it doesn't exactly encourage moderation. Many of us have been burned by an inability to give up something that guarantees pain in the end. When stuck in these bad patterns of behavior, we feed an appetite for destruction. Like zombies who climb over one another without regard or thoughtlessly walk off the edge of a cliff while pursuing their one desire, we can easily become blinded to the dangerous realities of an unchecked appetite.

I have a little dog who often acts like a zombie during daily walks as I follow behind him with green collection bags like some poor man's CSI agent. He doesn't like his leash. Sometimes he'll suddenly jump off the sidewalk to run across the street. He's pretty certain that cars are really fun toys to attack. One day, he darted into the street just as a pickup truck rounded the bend and headed toward us. I pulled on his leash hard enough to yank him off his feet. I didn't enjoy jerking him back like that, but he was safe. The alternative was watching him get destroyed because he

8. Quoted from Max Temkin's 2007 *Humans v. Zombies Documentary* filmed at Goucher College in Maryland where the game was created. The full documentary is on Vimeo at http://vimeo.com/1956330.

doesn't learn what I want to teach him and sometimes won't even respond to my voice when I call him. He wasn't hurt at all and went on sniffing and marking every square inch of the neighborhood, but I'm fascinated at how he can act so impulsively. No thought, just desire.

The really scary part is that we've seen people act like that. Their faces aren't empty in moments of untamable desire—their eyes blaze like wild animals. But worst of all is when we've been that person completely out of control and unable to suppress a terrible hunger that threatens those we love.

In an article for *First Things*, Ethan Cordray described the hunger this way:

> Zombies represent the appetite divorced from everything else. They are incapable of judgment, self-awareness, or self-preservation. Though they still move and act, they are not really alive. They hunger and are never filled. . . .
>
> . . . Without a soul to control it, the flesh is a slave to its own desires. The rise in popularity of zombies, then, may reflect a rise in anxiety over the elevation of appetite in modern life, a popular recognition that appetite has gotten out of control, and that unchecked, unreflective, and immoderate appetite is a form of death.[9]

I think Cordray is onto something here. Our fascination with zombies and the undead does have something to do with our culture's spiritual questions. Our search for meaning is a search to

9. Taken from "Zombies Are Us" by Ethan Cordray, August 15, 2011. Found at www.firstthings.com/onthesquare/2011/08/zombies-are-us

finally feel right. In reality most of the time we feel wrong some-how but don't even understand why. We're searching for a perfect moment of clarity to latch onto because the wrongness is somehow tied to confusion about existence. Even when we feel like we've got it all figured out for a minute those nagging doubts always manage to creep back up on us eventually.

EXISTING OR LIVING?

For me, the living characters in postapocalyptic stories are the real draw. They are the ones who represent the search for mean-ing. All that remains are a few relationships and threadbare faith as people struggle to find meaning in a survival existence. Their quest through a devastated world of the fallen is hard, frightening, confusing, and seemingly pointless—kind of the way real life can sometimes be. End-of-the-world stories feature empty cities and towns where anything can be had but nothing matters. All of the survivors have to come to grips with the world as it is, which is most definitely not how they want it.

We are fascinated because we can relate. Life is both a gift *and* a struggle. We wake and work and eat and sleep only to do it all over again the next day. Time is like an eraser of memories. We move on from one life event to the next—a wedding here and a funeral there; birthdays, promotions, vacations, and so on fill the gaps in between. Survivors in the movies move from one potential place of refuge to the next—a city that's been overrun or a military base that fell long ago—their hopes constantly reduced to pipe dreams as they chase false expectations. And it's their struggles with one another and within themselves along the way that we can connect with most powerfully. These zombie stories aren't horrific because of gory monsters but rather because we're confronted with the idea of an existence that is utterly meaningless.

I don't think there is anything scarier to me than the thought that life is absolutely meaningless. If that's true, then there is really nothing to live for. If that's true then I die now, a spiritual death that devours me from the inside and leaves me as nothing more than a zombie with a coffee mug in my hand morning after morning wondering what it even means to be alive. Merely existing is not living.

But I do believe in meaning and purpose even if a lot of my existence seems to take place somewhere between full confidence in and complete ignorance of God. Life isn't defined by extreme fear or faith but rather a quest to be fully alive during the simple blandness of routine days.

A lot of us may be physically alive yet dead inside. All we're really doing is existing, like spiritual zombies shambling away the days. I say "spiritual" because I believe there is more to us than flesh and bone. Something in us beyond science recognizes the power of things like love and beauty. It's that part of us—the soul, the mind, or whatever—that recognizes wrongness in our life, that knows there has to be more to life than this. It's the part of us that feels let down after we reach a destination we've been pursuing, like the survivors in *The Walking Dead* who finally reach Dr. Jenner at the Centers for Disease Control only to realize that *there are no answers.* We do the same thing when we walk into a bar or store or church hoping to get the fulfillment we seek only to walk away empty and disappointed. A lot of us keep trying to find answers in different places—or worse, in the same places—only to keep asking over and over again, *Why isn't this working?*

I've been trying to identify what this is for me. It's those things that were supposed to complete me and provide the satisfaction I always envisioned while growing up in some of the most comfortable conditions in world history.

This is the thing I always believed was part of the answer to life, as in I just need *this* to be happy and fulfilled. I used to think the magic *this* was academic success or a great job. Then I tried finding the right spouse.

Many people don't stop there, so they go after the perfect family (or at least the perfect-looking family).[10] We try all kinds of things in hopes of finding the right *this.* Maybe you've tried a sweet house or your addiction of choice. When none of that works we fall back on whatever fun can be scared up on weekends. Most of that stuff is pretty sweet after all. But I wonder if we truly find any kind of ultimate fulfillment in any of these things or if we feel more like zombies, unfulfilled by either pursuing or obtaining the objects of our desire.

And so we continue to hop on the conveyor belt of existence and check off boxes of things to achieve and acquire in Western

---

10. I'm looking at you, you crazy Photoshopped family-picture-Facebook person. Your family is beautiful. We get it. But can we please see at least one bad hair day or something?

culture until one day reality smacks us in the head and forces us to start asking bigger questions about places where smartphones don't work.

Like the afterlife.

That's been my experience anyway.

Ancient people searched for meaning and purpose just as we still do today, sometimes in equally bizarre places and with bizarre stories of dead and undead, life and afterlife. In fact, modern fans of the macabre are not alone in finding meaning among monsters or in looking for the living among the dead. We have thousands of years of records from different people speaking different languages in completely different cultures, and they all developed creative stories to supplement the never-ending quest to find life beyond the grave. As we'll see in the next chapter, we're just history repeating itself.

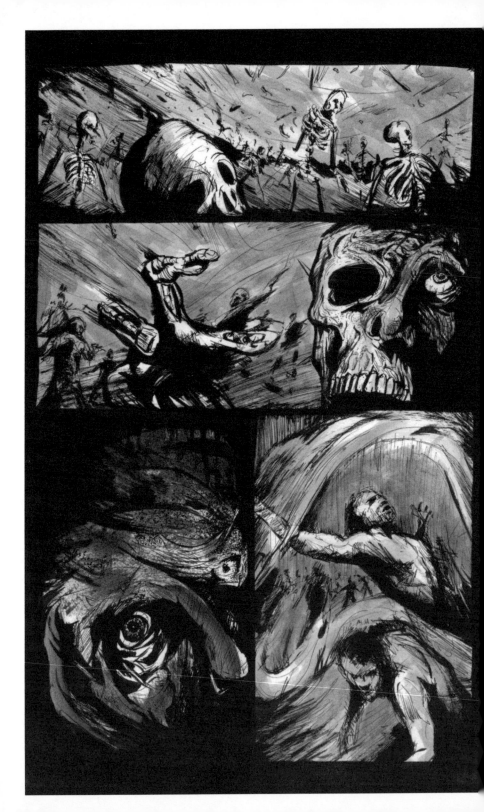

CHAPTER 2

THE ANCIENT UNDEAD

Every man dies. Not every man really lives.
—William Wallace, *Braveheart*

Humankind has searched for a way to overcome death since the beginning of recorded civilization. One of the most studied ancient writings, *The Epic of Gilgamesh*, chronicles the journey of a powerful king who loses his best friend Enkidu. He can't bear to bury the body because he knows that will be the end.

There's a remarkable passage in the epic that makes me think the living dead aren't such a new concept. The goddess Ishtar says:

I will knock down the Gates of the Netherworld,
I will smash the door posts, and leave the doors flat down,

and will let the dead go up to eat the living!

And the dead will outnumber the living! (Tablet VI)

That's some zombie mayhem talk way back in ancient Mesopotamia.

King Gilgamesh struggled with the prospect of his own mortality and traveled to the end of the earth in an attempt to conquer death. He ultimately failed, and humanity hasn't done any better four thousand years since.

The ancient Egyptians created massive pyramids to help send the recently deceased on his or her way. They were horrified of decay and believed the body had to be preserved in order for the soul to survive. The curse of the mummy has kept our attention ever since. I wanted to be an archaeologist when I was younger because nothing seemed cooler than searching for hidden tombs and undiscovered sarcophagi. Mummies fascinate us because they promise to hold secrets to the past. I grew up catching glimpses of old black-and-white films with typical mummies wrapped in strips of white cloth. Hollywood legend Bela Lugosi was usually involved. Brendan Fraser starred in the most hyped mummy film of recent times, though they played it as a quirky adventure rather than something frightening.

The most frightening mummy story I ever saw—and I'm sure it has something to do with that fact that I was young enough to still hear all those things going bump in the night—appeared in *Tales from the Darkside: The Movie*. Shot in anthology style, the film includes a featurette called "Lot 249," which was based on a short story published in 1892 by Sir Arthur Conan Doyle. A graduate student (Steve Buscemi) gets his hands on a mummy, which he controls enough to send it after some people he hates. The part I most remember is how that mummy killed a couple of victims by using ancient mummification techniques such as pulling a guy's brains out through his nose. Very educational stuff, really.

I recently read that in parts of Madagascar a dead person would be given a little entertainment for their afterlife journey.[1] Just before burial, someone would switch on a radio and place it in the coffin (apparently there is good reception in the afterlife). I think a really cruel joke would be to put on talk radio because you can't wish you were dead when you're already dead.

In more recent times, the history of Western civilization reveals a longing to receive contact from loved ones beyond the grave. This is understandable considering the millions of lives taken by the brutality of warfare over the past century and a half—especially the American Civil War and both World Wars. Unscrupulous hucksters have been more than happy to pose as clairvoyants capable of communicating with the dearly departed. As a result, nation after nation experienced a rise in spiritualism—particularly séances and occult practices—in the wake of these devastating conflicts.[2]

---

1. Michael Kerrigan, *The History of Death: Burial Customs and Funeral Rites, From the Ancient World to Modern Times* (Guilford, Conn.: Lyons Press, 2007), 25.

2. Magician Harry Houdini spent years on a personal crusade to expose these frauds. More on him in chapter 9.

UNDEAD IN THE BIBLE

The ancient Hebrews also had stories of life beyond the grave. Gritty references are scattered throughout the Old Testament, such as:

> Your dead will live;
>> Their corpses will rise.
> You who lie in the dust,
>> awake and shout for joy.
>>>> (Isaiah 26:19 NASB)

> For you will not leave my soul among the dead
>> or allow your holy one to rot in the grave.
>>> (Psalm 16:10 NLT)

> Many of those who sleep in the dust of the ground will awake, these to everlasting life, but the others to disgrace and everlasting contempt.
>> (Daniel 12:2 NASB)

> And after my skin has been destroyed,
>> yet in my flesh I will see God.
>>> (Job 19:26)

Some prophetic visions use creepy imagery to get a divine message across. The best example of such imagery comes from Ezekiel 37:

> Suddenly as I spoke, there was a rattling noise all across the valley. The bones of each body came together and attached them-

selves as they had been before. Then as I watched, muscles and flesh formed over the bones. Then skin formed to cover their bodies, but they still had no breath in them. Then he said to me, "Speak to the winds and say: 'This is what the Sovereign LORD says: Come, O breath, from the four winds! Breathe into these dead bodies so that they may live again.' " So I spoke as he commanded me, and the wind entered the bodies, and they began to breathe. They all came to life and stood up on their feet—a great army of them. (vv. 7-10 NLT)

There's one passage in the Old Testament that I call the Zombie Psalm. I could totally see the psalmist penning these words in ancient Israel as a horde of monsters closed in.

> Do not be afraid of the terrors of the night,
>> nor fear the dangers of the day,
>> nor dread the plague that stalks in darkness,
>> nor the disaster that strikes at midday.
> Though a thousand fall at your side,
>> though ten thousand are dying around you,
> these evils will not touch you. (Psalm 91:5-7 NLT)

It's striking that some of the oldest sources in recorded history include macabre descriptions of living corpses. The horror genre seems to have been around for a long time. From three thousand years ago, tales of the living dead such as these are recorded in the Torah and elsewhere in the Old Testament.

DEAD MAN'S BONES

The prophet Elisha spent his life in holy service, often revealing the loving side of his God through compassionate acts in the lives of needy individuals. He eventually died and was buried, and sometime later, a group of Israelites were burying a dead man from their community. While they labored to prepare a new grave they caught site of a band of raiders from Moab coming their way. These Moabites were frightening bandits who were known for storming into the area to pillage and plunder (2 Kings 13:20-21).

The Israelite burial crew panicked and chucked the dead man's body into Elisha's tomb. When the corpse touched Elisha's bones, the man came to life and stood up on his feet. That sight had to be even more frightening than the raiders. The Bible doesn't say, but I like to imagine those Moabites coming around the bend only to see a corpse standing in their way. Maybe the scene ended up looking more like a comedy than a horror movie. Those invaders must have looked like the keystone cops tripping over one another to get away from the walking dead guy.

The passage abruptly ends, so you might think that the resuscitated man just did a couple of laps in front of the Moabites before dropping dead again, but that's not likely. This man appears to be an Old Testament recipient of a second chance at life. He would have walked home to his family. I'll bet his wife or mom swooned when he came through the door and asked what they were having for dinner.

SHUNAMMITE WOMAN

Elisha was a fitting character for such a wild story since he was one of only two people in the Old Testament used by God to bring someone back to life.

In 2 Kings, we read the story of a Shunammite woman. She lived comfortably in her hometown of Shunem in northern Israel, not far from where the Jordan River and the Sea of Galilee converged. This kind lady went out of her way to care for Elisha and his servant, Gehazi. At first she fed him if he stopped by while traveling through the region. Before long she arranged a room on her roof, complete with a bed and lamp, for him. If they were around today, I bet she would've even got him a Snuggie. That rooftop man cave would've been quite a luxurious spot for Elisha since the life of a prophet included plenty of discomfort. God rewarded her service by blessing her with a son. The boy grew up and went to work in the fields, but tragedy struck one morning and he suddenly died.[3]

Devastated but not deterred, the Shunammite woman set out to find Elisha at Mount Carmel. The prophet felt terrible for her and instantly dispatched his servant to take his staff and lay it across the boy's face. When Elisha and the woman caught up, Gehazi explained that the staff did nothing to revive the boy.

When he finally arrived at the house, Elisha found the dead boy on his bed. He shut the door and prayed. Then he lay on the corpse and stretched out, hands to hands, eyes to eyes, mouth to

---

3. The boy went out to visit his father in the fields before suddenly exclaiming that his head hurt. He was taken back home and died by noontime (2 Kings 4).

mouth. As freaky as it sounds, the boy's body began to grow warm.[4] Elisha paced around the room a bit and then repeated the process. The boy suddenly sneezed seven times and opened his eyes! That sounds creepy enough to be in a spine-tingling thriller—the boy who was allergic to death.

Elisha wasn't the first prophet to be used by God for the purpose of raising someone from the dead, though. His forerunner and mentor Elijah also had a showdown with death.

THE WIDOW AT ZAREPHATH

When Elijah wasn't carrying out the messages and miracles of God, the great prophet tended toward isolation and despair. Elijah was a loner, but sometimes God had other plans and on one occasion sent him far north, to a town called Zarephath on the shore of the Mediterranean Sea. This land was essentially enemy territory near Sidon, the home of Jezebel, a Phoenician princess often considered to be the most evil woman in the entire Bible.

Elijah faithfully followed God's mission to find a widow in that town. The poor woman was down to the last of her food reserves. With only a bit of flour and oil left, she was preparing her last loaf of bread and then expected to die of starvation along with her son. But when Elijah asked it of her, she gave him her last loaf. For her

---

4. This life-giving act is imitative of the way God is described as having breathed life into Adam after forming him from the ground (Genesis 2:7). It also reminds me of modern-day CPR, although this boy was already dead.

generosity and obedience, God rewarded her by replenishing her oil and flour day after day.

Still, life is never easy. Sometime later, while Elijah was still there, the widow's son became sick and died. The heartsick mother questioned God, but she wasn't the only one. Even Elijah cried out to heaven, "O LORD my God, have you brought tragedy also upon this widow I am staying with, by causing her son to die?" (1 Kings 17:20).

Elijah took the dead boy to the upper room where he stayed, laid the body on the bed, and pleaded with God. He then stretched himself out across the corpse three times, just like his successor Elisha would later do for the Shunammite woman's son. In a loud cry that the widow must have heard from the floor below, Elijah said, "O LORD my God, let this boy's life return to him!" (v. 21).

God rewarded the faithful act, and the boy lived. Elijah carried the child back into the house and handed him over to the woman. Her sorrowful expression gave way to disbelief and then joy. It's hard to imagine a more dramatic scene in the life of an ordinary person. Zarephath meant "a place of testing," and it was. Elijah and the obedient woman passed their trial and honored God, who went so far as to suspend the power of death on their behalf.

DO YOU BELIEVE IN MIRACLES?

When I read these stories and consider our popular myths of the undead, I wonder how many people really believe in miracles.

According to researcher George Barna, "Most Americans, even those who say they are Christian, have doubts about the intrusion of the supernatural into the natural world."[5] That means a lot of people, skeptics and churchgoers alike, struggle with the idea of miracles and whether or not they're really possible. Dead people returning to life falls into the miraculous category, so what is one to think?

Struggling with the reality of supernatural events as they are recorded in the Bible is normal. Barna says that even those who follow Jesus struggle with the possibility of miracles. I find that interesting since Jesus isn't very special if miracles don't happen. You can't have Christianity without Jesus, as far as I can reason, and you can't have Christ without at least one very significant miracle: the Resurrection. A Christian who doesn't believe in miracles seems like a human who doesn't believe in birth.

Maybe the presence of so much technology and advanced science in our lives has undermined the possibility of the miraculous. When we come across events that have no scientific or natural explanation, we use a fancy word to describe them: *unexplainable*. A naturalist says that every phenomenon has a rational explanation even if we don't know what it is, but this understanding of the unexplained seems to require just as much faith as a belief in divine causation. There's simply a lot we don't know. Something caused the universe with all its natural laws to exist, yet it's unexplainable. The best we can manage are some theories. Most con-

---

5. The Barna Group, "Most American Christians Do Not Believe that Satan or the Holy Spirit Exist," April 10, 2009. www.barna.org/barna-update/article/12-faithspirituality/260-most-american-christians-do-not-believe-that-Satan-or-the-Holy-Spirit-exis.

servative Christians don't like to consider any other possibility outside of God creating all of existence in six literal days, although I think it's possible that the origins of the universe aren't as squeaky clean as that. However, a lot of naturalists are content to simply declare theories essentially claiming that nothing created everything.

I am not a scientist, but I do think it's logical to believe in a transcendent being who is behind an orderly and precise creation in which objective moral values exist whether we like them or not. Like many people throughout history, I call that transcendent being God. If this God created everything then it makes sense to me that the same being has the power to manipulate any law in the system he/she/it wants—death included.

So I may not be a scientist, but I also don't believe in chance. At least I don't believe that chance or luck has any power to make things happen. It can't. I'm a fan of Albert Einstein's maxim that "God does not play dice with the universe."[6]

I say all of this because much of this book is about miraculous events and the supernatural. Each one of us has to decide whether such cases are unexplainable or natural events or if the master of the universe just breaks some of the rules from time to time. I happen to believe in the latter. I don't have it all figured out, but I try to understand a little bit more here and there. We might actually make our lives a lot happier if we all started believing, at least, that we don't know everything.

---

6. This famous quote came from an exchange with legendary physicist Neils Bohr. Einstein believed that the universe was not random but predictable.

We take a lot for granted when we learn in a vacuum. Our tendency is to get comfortable and stay there, so we often get encased in bubbles where we're surrounded by others who reaffirm our beliefs rather than challenging us. I remember objecting to something a professor said during a class in my first month ever of college. As soon as I told him he was wrong he asked me why. I instantly realized that the best response I could come up with boiled down to saying something about how I had never been taught any different. That's a great response if you're Forrest Gump, not so great at university.

One of the best things that ever happened to me was realizing how much I didn't know. Feeling as though we have to be right all the time is exhausting. A lot of preprogramming had to be stripped out of me, which is frustrating, painful even, but the results are worthwhile. For one, I don't think my faith is as flat as it was for so much of my life. Easy answers and clichés get really boring after a while and are certainly nothing to base an entire spiritual outlook on.

When we give up the need to know everything, we find how much more interesting it is to talk with people. Conversations become fun again. For instance, I've had some with people who think I'm crazy for believing in God but who also are seriously concerned about an outbreak of zombies who will eat everybody. Zombies are scientific, they say. God is not. I tell them that I think God made science and could use zombies to violate natural laws. The Bible is already filled with enough wildly bizarre happenings that I don't think zombies would be that much more shocking.

Every answer we ever seek will lie somewhere within the possibilities we are able to see. Conclusions must be clear, but they are more likely to be wrapped in mystery than in clichés.

MASKING DEATH

There are family photos on the wall at my mom's house. A couple of them are very formal, taken before I was born, and you can tell that getting such a picture was a big event. We often take group pictures to commemorate events. Call me morbid, but I always think about how helpful those images will be after some of the people in them are dead. I imagine people who aren't even born yet looking at a picture of me someday and being surprised at how I actually looked and how it differs from some perspective they developed through stories about me. Everyone wants to live on, to be remembered. We're fortunate to be able to remember one another this way. People have always wanted to take photos; they just didn't know it would be possible until the nineteenth century. Instead, they carved images on cave walls, sketched pictures, and created vibrant paintings.

Throughout prior centuries, death masks were even crafted by making plaster molds of people's faces after they died. Those things are pretty eerie but made sense before photography. The coolest death mask ever probably belonged to King Tut, the legendary Egyptian pharaoh whose treasured tomb was discovered in

1922, but that one is much more ornamental and not as lifelike as most of them.[7]

It's strange how some of us get into mementos of the dead, but we do. Well, history nerds like me do anyway. I actually own a piece of Alexander Hamilton's hair. He's the guy on the ten-dollar bill and one of my favorite Americans ever. He's also been dead for more than two hundred years. You know your big sister loves you when she gives you a piece of Alexander Hamilton's hair for Christmas. Some of my friends are skeptical about it really being a piece of his hair, but I hope they're wrong because that would be embarrassing after all the bragging I've done. Actually, most people aren't as impressed with my Alexander Hamilton hair as I think they should be.

As I write about ancient people and death and consider the meaning of mementos of the dead, I wonder what it would be like if we took measures to commemorate our *spiritual* death as well— that emptiness of mere existence combined with our failures that leave us hollow and scarred. What if we were to take pictures of our ugliest moments and build monuments to the places and times in which we really blew it.

But that's not what we do. I doubt I'm the only person who's ever burned a picture of a moment in time I wish would vanish. We might be able to eradicate some evidence, but the memory remains. Sometimes our biggest failures are foremost in our minds.

---

7. Do a simple Google image search on "death masks" and you'll see plaster freeze-frames of people from William Shakespeare to Abraham Lincoln. It's either really cool or extremely creepy depending on your tastes.

Voices whisper our unworthiness, mistakes are amplified in our memories, and our worst fears come true when someone throws our past failings in our faces.

But if we let that paralyze us too much, we might be mistaken for already dead and be buried alive.

Whether physical or spiritual, death isn't something we like to remember. We should remember that one of the main reasons for creating death masks was so portraits or statues could be accurately created later on. The disturbing memory of death was used to create a legacy of life. I don't think we should build monuments to our failures, but if we can't erase them from memory, they should at least be used to further illuminate light in the darkness.

Even Gilgamesh managed to finally come around some at the end of his epic journey. Despite all the despair he felt over his own mortality and the intense grief of losing his friend—not to mention Ishtar's threats that dead people would eat the living—the king finally accepted reality and was able to put aside the painful face of death in order to see some of the positive aspects of his legacy. That is how most stories end after all. Someone dies. We mourn and move on. Not so with zombies and vampires or even real people according to some of these ancient accounts. But the Bible has a second half. Turns out that guys like Elijah, Elisha, and Ezekiel were just the beginning. The New Testament records seven separate instances in which dead people came back to life. The first of these fascinating tales is about a woman who lost everything before the answer to a question that she probably didn't even ask showed up.

CHAPTER 3

THE OUTCAST

Widow. The word consumes itself.

—Sylvia Plath

My family accidentally left me at a funeral home when I was four years old. I was lost, surrounded by strangers in dark rooms. Lost, Strangers, Darkness—LSD for kids. The trifecta of childhood terror. Throw a dead person into the middle of that room and we're set up for a fun little side effect I like to call life scars. Amazingly, my reaction didn't include stains on my dress pants; over the years, I would manage to rebuild courage from that small victory.

So there I stood, frightened yet determined to locate any member of my family—I would even settle for one of my sisters.

But locating them required a full sweep of the establishment. I'd have to approach the you-know-what. The *dead person*.

Trembling, I moved about the room. The thought crossed my mind that I might never see my family ever again. And that's the problem with the concept of forever. The stakes are just too high. I had to find my family even if it meant approaching the crowd gathered around the big box with a dead person inside. When I stepped forward, somehow the room turned even darker, which led to a disturbing phenomenon in which the brightest part of the room was the exact spot where the dead body lay.

Closer and closer I moved toward the body when I realized something that every little kid instinctively knows. *Corpses always lunge at you.* That's the trouble with dead people. They always come back to life when you least expect it. I began to panic and froze in my tracks. My only chance was to be as still as possible and not even make a sound. With any luck I might turn invisible. But it didn't work, and I took off. I ended up at the other end of the building in front of a massive window through which glorious sunlight made my tear-stained cheeks gleam.

Eventually some teenager found me and calmed me down. I'm sure he explained that my family hadn't left me to live in the funeral home with dead people who would eat me by nightfall. By the time my family pulled up in front of the place, that guy and I were just hanging out on the front steps.

We've often reminisced about that day with laughter. The whole ordeal was an honest mistake. Our family had one of those station wagons from the 1980s, very hearselike, with an acre of space behind the backseat in an era with no seatbelt laws. My older sisters had apparently indicated that little brother was somewhere back there and off the family had rolled, leaving little me behind. I guess it sounds pretty bad, but what's an afternoon of terror compared to a lifetime of laughter? And therapy.[1]

Ironically, I ended up taking a job at a cemetery during high school and college, and throughout those years of working in the graveyard I observed a lot of funerals and countless mourners. I've seen people grieve in different ways—some funerals were celebratory, others were casual and chatty because, after all, the deceased was suffering for so long and had a good full life. And then there are those shocking deaths, the ones that leave us breathless and desperate.

Sudden heart attacks.

Random violence.

Tragic accidents.

But the worst pain a human can endure, I believe, is the loss of a child. No one should have to bury a son or daughter, yet many parents have faced the awful dread of seeing their child in a casket, a life tragically cut short. A woman in the ancient town of Nain went through that horrible experience more than two thousand years ago as a mysterious teacher rolled into town. The Gospel of Luke relays the story of the widow's personal tragedy.

TWO CROWDS AT A CROSSROADS

Luke is the only gospel writer to chronicle this amazing story. After leaving Capernaum, Jesus and his disciples arrive at Nain and

---

1. I'm kidding.

encounter a sorrowful scene. "As he approached the town gate, a dead person was being carried out—the only son of his mother, and she was a widow. And a large crowd from the town was with her" (Luke 7:12).

This poor woman, already widowed, loses her only son, which makes her situation pretty desperate in first-century Palestine. Her son would have been the man who provided for her. He would have become the man of the house—a caretaker able to work in the field, fix a leaking roof, and move heavy objects. He would have given her emotional strength and lifted her spirits when depression set in. In his face, she would still have been able to see a part of the husband she had lost.

The pain of struggling to go on was only compounded by fears of the future. Imagine her overwhelming despair and the questions perforating her thoughts. She was filled with pleas and left with no answers. As the hours melted away she wondered, *What will I do now?*

But this story isn't so much about the widow. It is very much about the dead man.

Luke never says how he died. Scholars and artists throughout the centuries portray him as an adult male, likely a twenty-something. In any case he died young.[2] We've all had to face the possibility of our own deaths, but none of us ever plan on it. We grow

---

2. Ancient Jewish funeral customs varied depending on the age of the deceased. Babies under one month old were carried out against someone's chest. If a full month to one year old they were placed in a little coffin and carried in someone's arms. One- to three-year-olds were carried in a coffin on the shoulders. Three-year-olds and up were carried out on a bier or bed.

up and go through our school years thinking about life and planning for an abstract future. Lots of things might happen, but death is rarely expected. Dying is something reserved for *old age*. But then tragedy strikes, and if you've experienced this before, you know how your mind brings everything into focus. Suddenly nothing else matters. Plans and petty distractions become insignificant. Objects of daily attention are stripped of meaning.

Whatever the circumstances of this man's death, he lost the battle and his mother found herself alone in the valley of the shadow of death. On the day of the funeral, a large crowd gathered with her, the amount of vocal mourners indicating respect for the deceased. Work in the town would have stopped for the day. The dead had to be buried a considerable distance from the city, so a funeral procession would have to carry the corpse the entire way. Pall bearers switched off to alleviate the weight of the bier or bed upon which the young man was laid.

Picture the woman there in the hot desert sun. She's crying so hard that her throat hurts. It's hard to believe she even has anymore tears left to shed, yet they stream down her cheek like liquid prayers. She cakes a little more dirt on her careworn face with each wipe of her hand; no one can console her, nothing can be said that will make the situation any better. As hopeless as the reality seems, it's nothing compared to the pain ripping her heart apart. Every area of her life is now defined by need. No one can help her.

And that's when this miracle worker from Galilee named Jesus shows up. The crowd following him is giddy and jubilant, replaying stories about amazing things he had been doing all over the region. As they arrive at the town gate of Nain, they collide with the grief and mourning of this funeral. Jesus stands in the middle of this strange intersection waiting for their encounter.

I'm reminded of one of my favorite movies of all time, *The Princess Bride*. After some torture in the Pit of Despair, our hero Westley dies. His crestfallen friends Inigo and Fezzik take the body to the home of Miracle Max (played by Billy Crystal). As Westley lay lifeless on a table, Max tells the visitors that "It just so happens that your friend here is only mostly dead. There's a big difference between mostly dead and all dead. *Mostly* dead is slightly alive."[3]

I don't mean that Jesus makes me think of Billy Crystal in old-man makeup (although they are both Jewish). But Jesus did have that easy-going attitude around dead people that seemed to say, *Sure this is bad, but it's not like it's the end of the world or anything.* Also, sometimes the good guy gets to come back from the dead, so it's not always about horrible monsters.

WHAT GOD SEES

The noise of both crowds quiets as the woman and Jesus meet. Observers on each side move forward to see what is happening. Luke says, "When the Lord saw her, his heart went out to her and he said, 'Don't cry'" (Luke 7:13).

---

3. If you've never seen *The Princess Bride* then your life is not complete. Go find a copy right now.

Jesus *sees* her. So much depth in that simple phrase. It's as if he didn't just see a woman crying at a funeral but knew her entire situation. It's as if he knew how desperate her reality was and even saw what no one else could: the invisible scars.

To me, spiritual deadness has something to do with turmoil inside of us that we can only feel for ourselves. We harbor unspoken words in our minds and hide private pain and secret shame that is often undiscovered by anyone else including our closest friends. Some longings are buried so deep inside of us that we can't even express them, and in some cases we don't even know they are there. It's all part of the wrongness we sense that I described in the first chapter. Holding onto something that others can't know about is often unbearable. Those secrets are heavy burdens to carry alone, especially when you feel like there's no one else to help you lift the weight that is trapping you. The idea of a "God who sees" is the idea that we're never alone.

I don't think God just glances around, noticing different people here and there. The only idea of God that can make sense to us is one who is fully present and aware and knowledgeable. We can't get our minds around the perspective of God, but perhaps he[4] has already stood at the end of what we call time and looked back upon all of existence, and if that's true then God could also look down from outside of time and see the whole story at once, from beginning to end.

---

4. Although I often use the masculine pronoun to describe God, I believe that we are all made in his image, men and women alike. To me that means God contains all feminine traits as well.

The frustrating thing about that idea is that it confirms an all-powerful cosmic deity who sees everything including pain and evil yet lets it happen anyway. Philosophers and theologians have been debating this topic for centuries. I don't have anything ground-breaking to add here, so I'll just go ahead trying to accept it for now even though I admittedly don't really understand or even like it.

The reason I choose to accept these hard ideas about God is because I also see loving acts coming from him that I can't live without. For example, despite such amazing power and limitless understanding, God still cares enough to look down and see me. Just like the poor widow at Nain, we sometimes feel as though our world is caving in, like there's no hope, like no one cares. But in those moments we feel that God sees us and never worries. I wonder if we wouldn't be better off considering God's perspective more.

Luke says not only that Jesus saw her but also that his heart went out to the woman. God doesn't just see us as we are only to leave us there. Instead, he is moved to the depth of his being and *does something*. True compassion is more than just feeling sorry for someone or saying that suffering is terrible. There's action involved. Jesus cared about the widow's pain and did something about it. I doubt any of us would look at a grieving mother leaning over the corpse of one of her kids and say, "don't cry," but Jesus did. Seems like an awfully harsh thing to say, unless he has the power to change her situation.

So Jesus was a funeral crasher. He touched the coffin, and the pallbearers froze. Remember, even at four years of age I could have told you that this is the moment in a scary movie where the corpse will lunge at you. An interruption like this was even more shocking in the first century when ceremonial cleanliness meant so much. Touching a corpse might still be freaky these days, but Jewish people back then feared the disgrace of being labeled unclean, a social stigma that meant exclusion from the Temple and separation from others. But the drama of the moment overwhelmed the culture shock. The disciples probably gave each other sideways glances and wondered what their rabbi was doing.

DEAD MAN'S PARTY

I've been a pallbearer for a lot of people, from close loved ones to distant relatives to many people I never met. The reason I've carried dozens of bodies is because that's what you do when you work at a cemetery and also come from a small family short on able-bodied men. Plus there was that whole abandoned-at-the-funeral-home experience as a small child, so I guess I got some of the apprehension about corpses out of the way early. I've served as a pallbearer enough to know where I should stand—back right. *Back* because I'm the tallest and you need symmetry for these kinds of things, and *right* because I'm left-handed and prefer to use my stronger arm.[5] Sometimes the job takes more work than normal, and I try to figure out who's not carrying his or her weight.

---

5. We may all come into the world the same way but most definitely do not go out the same. Some corpses are heftier than others. Pallbearing is like zombie hunting—you'll want to limber up first.

It's a serious moment, but you can't help contemplating these sorts of things.

It's always a short and easy trip from the funeral home to the hearse, but you never know what will happen after that. I live in southwestern Pennsylvania where precipitation and hills are common. Some rookie pallbearers will wear dress shoes with slick bottoms, but that's a mistake—you want to get some traction or else one of those disasters that only happens in screwball comedies will take place. No one wants to see the casket dropped and flying open unless you are watching a Monty Python movie.

One thing that usually *doesn't* happen is someone stepping in front of the procession and stopping it. So I can imagine how confused some of those people must have been when some random guy stopped the procession. All of these people from Nain were walking to the graveyard when Jesus stepped in and with one gesture seemed to say, "Not so fast, folks."

Then he spoke. "Young man, I say to you, get up!" (Luke 7:14). His disciples and followers had apparently not heard anything like this yet. Sure, he'd healed some disabled and blind people, but talking to corpses? We can't imagine how suspenseful that moment must have been.

The man sat up and began to talk. Began to talk? What would a dead man have to say right after being brought back to life? He was definitely having one of the all-time weirdest days ever after all. I bet Jesus had a big ol' grin on his face as he gave the young man back to his mother. Luke says that the people watching the scene in Nain were filled with awe, and no wonder! The mourners turned to cheerers as a party broke out in the streets of the town. This story is the only recorded time that Jesus raised a dead person during the actual funeral.

The French painter Pierre Bouillon (1776–1831) created one of the best depictions from the New Testament that I've seen when he took on this scene in *Jésus ressuscitant le fils de la veuve de Naïm* (Jesus raising the son of the widow of Nain). The first thing that stands out is the young man sitting up as he returns to life. For one, his skin is green. He's throwing a sheet off of him, which leaves his arms positioned in something close to a classic zombie pose. It just looks cool. The second thing I see is the various reactions of the onlookers. You can almost tell what each figure is thinking in the moment. Some want a closer look whereas a couple step back. One man seems repulsed. While everyone else stares at the widow's son, this man recoils and glares at Jesus. No matter how each witness feels about what they've just seen, you know that they will all be talking about it.

News tends to get around pretty quickly when dead people come back to life. Witnesses of the miracle spread the word about a new prophet sent by God to help the people, and residents of Nain saw extra significance in this miracle. The story from the last chapter about Elisha raising the Shunammite woman's son from the dead took place on the other side of the hill from where this widow and her son lived. The news made such a splash that John the Baptist even heard what happened from a prison cell about eighty miles away (Luke 7:18-23).

OUTCASTS

One of the unique things about the miracle at Nain is how Jesus raised the widow's son from the dead without being asked. He was constantly being pressured, followed, and chased by thousands, but for this despairing widow he took the initiative without a petition.

The Old Testament repeatedly describes God's loving care for the most desperate of all people, namely widows and orphans. It's no coincidence that Luke is the only gospel writer to record the story of this widow. He may have been a doctor as well as a gifted writer, but he understood what being an outcast was about. Many people think of Luke as one of the twelve disciples, but he wasn't. In fact, a lot of scholars believe he wasn't even Jewish, which would likely make him the only Gentile writer of the Bible, a man known for including stories of social outcasts. Luke is the only gospel writer to include the story of the prodigal son (Luke 15:11-32) or the thief who repented on the cross next to Jesus. Luke alone describes repentance and acceptance of wicked tax collectors such as Zacchaeus. And the good doctor, who also wrote the book of Acts, recorded the tale of the good Samaritan when no one else did. No surprise then that Luke highlights the unique care Jesus demonstrated for women in an extremely male-dominated society.

Less than two chapters later in Luke, we see at least five separate incidents of Jesus specifically helping women, and two of these scenes involve people coming back to life. After the scene with the widow of Nain, Luke describes the sinful woman who anointed Jesus' feet. In the very next passage he records how women accompanied Jesus and the disciples. Later in that same chapter he recounts how Jesus healed the bleeding woman and brought Jairus's daughter back to life.

Often, Christian churches are accused of being sexist, and it's often true. If there's one place in this world where people shouldn't be excluded or made to feel like outsiders, it's the church. Unfortunately, Jesus is often judged based on things his imperfect followers have done. But Jesus' life reveals a much different attitude toward the powerless, those without a voice. Jesus didn't discriminate when someone needed help. Jesus paints a picture of a community that is aware and sensitive to the needs of socially stigmatized individuals rather than one that continues to marginalize them.

We see this amazing connection between Jesus and women throughout the rest of the New Testament as well. He shows love to the woman at the well who's used to being treated as a prostitute walking around with a "kick me" sign on her back. When an adulterous woman is caught in the act and thrown at the feet of Jesus, he defends her life and intimidates her accusers. And Jesus of course loved his mother, Mary. He even had at least two sisters according to Matthew.[6] (The image of Jesus as a big brother isn't one the Scriptures dwell on, nor do we often think about it, but we should picture him laughing and shaking his head while his little sisters bickered over the silly things little sisters bicker about.)

6. "Coming to his hometown, [Jesus] began teaching the people in their synagogue, and they were amazed. 'Where did this man get this wisdom? Isn't his mother's name Mary, and aren't his brothers James, Joseph, Simon and Judas? *Aren't all his sisters with us?*' " (Matthew 13:54-56, emphasis mine).

One of the worst things about being an outcast is the pain of rejection. Often we are dominated by a need for acceptance, whether we admit it to ourselves or not. I didn't realize it for many years, but I felt it. I was the class clown who desperately wanted to be in cool places with cool people. Slights by peers hurt, especially when those people defined my identity. The sad part is that in my pursuit to obtain the status I craved, I pushed away spiritual identity in God, the only one who has never rejected me. It wasn't that I didn't believe in God; I just ignored him. Jesus didn't just love outcasts. He *became* an outcast who knew what it was like to be hated and despised. But despite all that, he knew exactly who he was. His identity came from God and no one could mess with that. He stood against the holier-than-thou crowd and made his acceptance of everyone very clear when he said, "whoever comes to me I will *never* drive away" (John 6:37, emphasis mine).

Regardless of the standard set before us, a lot of us are held back by a belief that we somehow aren't good enough. That lie is a killer because it puts distance between us and whomever we are seeking a relationship with. In God's eyes we are not defined by whatever regrettable things we've done in the past. He looks at us just as Jesus looked at the woman caught in adultery: with love rather than rejection.

I can relate to the widow of Nain because she was sinking in the death around her, yet Jesus showed up and offered her life. She didn't even have to ask. He was there loving her before she ever knew it.

I heard a great speaker named Louie Giglio talk about this

widow's story. He said we don't know how close they were to the place of the young man's burial, but he was about to be thrown into a hole, dead and buried. Louie says that a lot of us are spiritually on a stretcher being carried out of town. We allow things in our lives that are killing our connection to God, and it's almost over for us. We're so dead that we can't help ourselves at all. But just then Jesus intersects our lives, reaches out to us, and says "Stop. There's not going to be a funeral here today."[7]

I love that God is a funeral crasher.

That's what happened in Nain. A corpse was being carried out of town, but then Jesus arrived, and the funeral turned into a dead man's party. That man came back to life and danced home. It must have been even more exciting than seeing your family pull up in a station wagon in front of a funeral home that you were left at when you were four years old.

Word spread throughout Judea, Galilee, and beyond and even reached the town of a synagogue ruler named Jairus whose own child was about to suffer the same terrible fate of the widow's son.

7. This talk was given at the 2012 Passion Conference in Atlanta. For more info go to www.268generation.com.

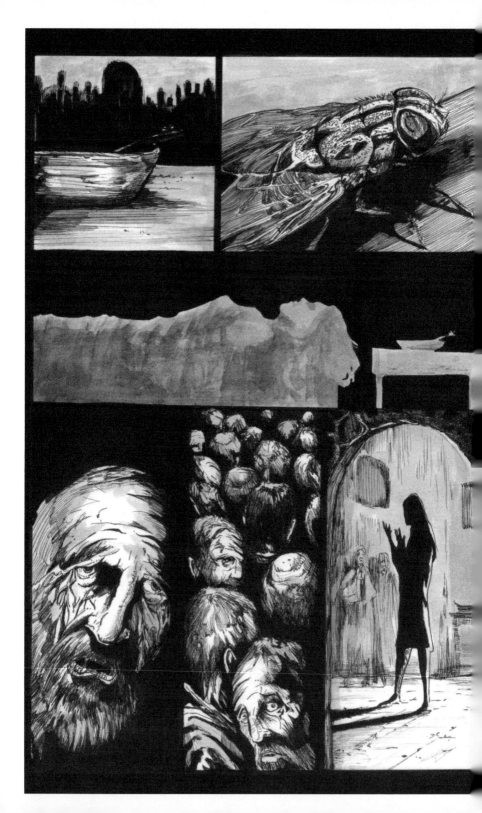

CHAPTER 4

THE RULER

Men fear death as children fear to go in the dark; and as that

natural fear in children is increased by tales, so is the other.

—Francis Bacon[1]

Y ou've probably seen movies with those suspenseful Look-out-behind-you! moments in which everybody watching the movie plus anyone who's not even really paying attention sees the danger bearing down on the protagonist. The only person who doesn't realize that anything is wrong is the fictional character we hate ourselves for caring about because how could they be so *stupid*? A lot of times these villains creep up from behind after they were

---

1. No relation to Kevin. Probably.

supposedly killed anywhere from one to seventeen times. In *Zombieland*, a savvy fighter of the undead named Columbus follows one rule especially designed to avoid those embarrassing, and deadly, instances in which the zombie you just supposedly killed gets back up and eats you. It's called double tap. Don't take any chances. Put a second bullet in those monsters even after you're pretty sure the job is done because zombies are really bad about staying dead.

One particular Look-out-behind-you! moment that stands out in my mind happened in a movie called *Silence of the Lambs*. During the film's climax, authorities lose track of Hannibal Lecter's body. They thought that they had the entire police department watching him but it turns out that was just some guy whose face had been borrowed by the savage sociopath. Meanwhile, some poor guy is riding in an ambulance with what he thinks is a wounded officer. With his back turned, the officer's arms begin to move as he slowly rises from the gurney. At this point you know the guy on the walkie talkie with his back turned to the danger is doomed. You think, *You're going to just have to accept what's about to happen to you there, guy.* What happens is that Hannibal Lecter removes another person's face from his own in the most terrifying "Gotcha!" moment I've ever seen.[2]

Life imitates art, so maybe that's why we have so many stories of real people who were reportedly dead even though they were alive and kicking. Consider, for example, what happened to Joe

---

2. Then what else happens is you don't sleep well for the next three years.

DiMaggio—one of the greatest all-around baseball players who ever lived. During thirteen seasons he led the New York Yankees to nine world championships. The Yankee Clipper, as he was known, performed some remarkable athletic feats despite spending a couple of years serving in the Air Force during World War II, the prime of his career. He even married Marilyn Monroe along the way. Joltin' Joe had lived quite a life by 1999, so imagine his surprise one evening when he turned on his television to discover that he was dead.

An NBC technician had erroneously pushed a button that sent the report scrolling along the bottom of the screen that DiMaggio had died, and the hall of famer was reportedly furious over the mistake. Rightfully so! After all, he was in a deadly fight with lung cancer. He died for real just a few weeks later.

DiMaggio isn't the only notable figure whose death was wrongly reported. After reading the report of his death in a magazine, the British writer Rudyard Kipling reportedly penned this message to the publisher: "I've just read that I am dead. Don't forget to delete me from your list of subscribers."

One of the more bizarre incidents happened to Jamaican activist Marcus Garvey. After suffering a stroke in 1940, Garvey recuperated in England during the early days of World War II. One morning in June he came across a column in a Chicago newspaper that claimed he was dead. The article described him as a man who died "broke, alone, and unpopular." The news overwhelmed the 52-year-old man who suffered a second stroke and died the next morning.[3]

---

3. I'm pretty sure that's textbook irony.

A premature obituary may be partially responsible for the creation of the Nobel Peace Prize. In 1888, a French newspaper ran the news that Alfred Nobel had died when in fact his brother had passed away. The scathing headline read, "The merchant of death is dead." Soon after, Nobel came up with the famous peace prize in a successful attempt to put a positive spin on the family name.[4]

Television and newspapers aren't the only media to botch death reports. The famous CNN incident of 2003 created much confusion through a website error that allowed viewers to read obituary templates of international leaders. The partially written drafts included tributes to people like Pope John Paul II, Fidel Castro, Ronald Reagan, and more, all of whom were still alive at the time. One of the funniest errors was a reference to Vice President Dick Cheney as the "UK's favorite grandmother."

I remember listening to a hometown Pittsburgh Pirates baseball game one night in 1998 when radio announcer Lanny Frattare announced that James Earl Jones had died. We were stunned that the legendary actor and voice of Darth Vader was suddenly dead— only he wasn't. The announcer misunderstood the breaking news that James Earl *Ray,* assassin of Martin Luther King Jr., was the recently deceased.[5]

In November 2005, the *Pittsburgh Post-Gazette* mistakenly reported the death of historian Arthur Schlesinger Jr. who was still

---

4. There's a good article on Nobel's move toward peaceful ways called *Story of 'merchant of death' Alfred Nobel* on www.swedish wire.com.

5. On a zombie related note, we've been waiting for the Pirates to come back from the dead for twenty years now.

alive and kicking. The editors retracted the statement a couple of days later with this message: "We are embarrassed but happy for Mr. Schlesinger." My hometown seems to have problems with false death reports.

Premature obituaries can be pretty funny, except maybe not to the people suddenly being told they're dead. It turns out that the Bible has its own story of a premature obituary, sort of.

A WAITING ROOM IN GALILEE

The ministry of Jesus was on fire—he healed people, taught with authority, and raised the widow's son from the dead. Some people even heard about how he could control nature itself after he yelled at a violent storm and shut it down instantly.

One day a large crowd gathered on the banks of the Sea of Galilee as Jesus and his friends returned from the other side of the lake where Jesus had thrown evil spirits out of a tormented young man. The miracle worker was about to go to work, and his office was the familiar shoreline of Galilee.

A respected man of the town named Jairus stood amid the surging crowd. All he could think about was his twelve-year-old daughter who was gravely ill. No one could do anything about it, but Jairus couldn't let go of hope even as her life slipped away. Jairus served as an official of the local synagogue and knew about the ministry of Jesus that was so troublesome to his Pharisee acquaintances.

The official position of the local leadership was that the teacher from Nazareth had to be stopped. Jesus was a blasphemer, they said, and Jairus was likely expected to fall in line. Such an allegation threatened not only Jesus but anyone who followed him, and since the position Jairus held was an elected one, he would normally take care to act appropriately in public since those who cast votes were often around.

But he didn't care about his friends or colleagues anymore. They couldn't heal his dying daughter. Regardless of his power and position, Jairus was powerless and desperate. He lingered in that uncomfortable spot between uncertain hope and belief. Going to Jesus was no simple matter. He risked his standing in the community and even his entire livelihood to do so. He was desperate enough that he left his family at home on the worst day of their lives.

I imagine Jairus waiting there on the Galilean shore like a nervous parent in a hospital waiting room, pacing and stroking his beard. Geographically, the only spot on the planet lower than the one in which he stood was the Dead Sea. Death. Perhaps he thought of his daughter and felt the sudden stabs of loss already puncturing his heart.

When Jesus arrived onshore, Jairus knelt before him in the midst of all those onlookers and, without regard for popular opinion, pleaded for the life of his little girl. "My daughter is dying," he said. "Please come and put your hands on her so she will be healed and live" (Mark 5:23).

Jairus's desperate cry seemed to work because without hesitation Jesus said, "Let's go." But as they were on their way Jesus stopped suddenly, looked around, and asked, "Who touched me?"

WHO TOUCHED ME?

An eager crowd swarmed around Jesus as he accompanied the man to his house. Jesus was the first-century equivalent of a rock star, and the scene would have resembled a mosh pit: people jostling and pushing—and suddenly Jesus wants to know who touched him?

The disciples responded just as any of us would by saying, "What are you talking about?" Jesus ignored them and kept looking around, waiting for a specific individual to acknowledge the touch. Someone in that crowd knew what he knew—a hurting woman who quietly sought healing by touching Jesus' cloak.[6]

The woman's situation was terribly desperate. She was sick, suffering menstrual bleeding, both painful and humiliating, for twelve years. That's 4,380 days, enough time to get three college degrees or make it halfway to a silver wedding anniversary. It's also the number of years that Jairus's daughter had been alive. The illness had robbed her of some of the best years of her life. But there was even something worse than the physical pain and embarrassment of her situation. Jewish law stated that the bleeding made her ceremonially unclean. She couldn't stroll through the market

6. Matthew, Mark, and Luke each recount this story of Jairus and the bleeding woman. My favorite telling is found in Luke 8:40-56.

or attend wedding celebrations or worship in the synagogue. It was also common for Jewish men to avoid talking or even making eye contact with women so as to avoid violating their codes. Her condition meant not only that she was unclean but also that anybody she *touched* was defiled. The loneliness of her life must have caused extreme emotional pain. She was a social outcast, unable to be with her people. The poor, bleeding woman was barely a step above a leper. The legal codes were so strict that the bleeding woman couldn't even have a husband. I heard Beth Moore explain that no man would have married the bleeding woman if she had contracted this disease when she was single, and if she was married when she got sick then her husband would have divorced her.[7]

She was a woman without hope who chose to reach out and touch Jesus because of uncertain belief that she might be healed. The risk, of course, was that she would defile Jesus with her touch causing him to lash out in anger over her unlawful action.

One of the less obvious ironies of this story is that this unclean woman arrived as Jesus was walking with one of the rulers of the synagogue. Part of Jairus's job included securing the sanctity of the culture. For years he was responsible for dealing with the people in the region on many matters including ceremonial cleanliness. The Bible doesn't say, but it's certainly possible that Jairus knew this woman or was at least familiar with her situation.

Jesus announced to the entire crowd that this "unclean" woman had touched him, and after the woman explained herself,

---

7. This talk was given at the 2012 Passion Conference in Atlanta. For more info go to www.268generation.com.

Jesus said, "Daughter, your faith has healed you. Go in peace and be freed from your suffering" (Mark 5:34).

In this powerful statement we can discover an aspect of God that is deeply personal. First, Jesus said that the woman is healed because of her faith and not as a result of touching the hem of Jesus' garment. His cloak was unnecessary for her healing. The power was not in the clothing Jesus wore but in the grace he offered as a response to the woman's faith. Often we mistake symbols for the reality to which they point. A second significant point of note is how fully Jesus accepts the woman; he calls her daughter with a love that mirrors the affection that Jairus has for his little girl. As he did with the widow from Nain, Jesus offers this woman personal value by healing and adopting her.

Throughout the entire exchange between Jesus and the bleeding woman, Jairus stands by, a mixture of sorrow and awe most likely stirring within him. He understands better than most what being a loving father is all about, equal parts joy and pain. Right now, pain is winning but perhaps hope begins to take hold in his heart. The one person in the entire universe who can heal his baby is right next him, kind and able, as he demonstrates with the bleeding woman. *Maybe Jesus really could take away death,* Jairus might be thinking.

Just then, however, someone from the house of Jairus arrives with soul-crushing news.

"Your daughter is dead," the man says.

JUST BELIEVE

Jairus's friends tell him that it is time to call off the rescue effort. What a punch in the gut that must have been for him—his worst fear come true. As he struggles to process the news, he turns his vacant gaze toward Jesus, who meets him with a stare as piercing as his words: "Don't be afraid. Just believe."

The wails of mourners and drones of flutes drift toward them as they approach Jarius's home. Silence during death was seen as disrespectful in the first-century Jewish culture, and some people even worked as professional mourners who were paid to bring the sadness.[8]

Always one to ask puzzling questions, Jesus entered the house and asked why everyone was crying. I'm not sure what the Aramaic word is for "duh!" but they probably said it. As if that wasn't odd and perhaps disrespectful enough, Jesus told them that the little girl wasn't dead but rather sleeping.

And then they laughed at him.

Jesus responded by calmly throwing them all out of the house.

Once the house was quieted, Jesus, Peter, James, and John followed Jairus and his wife into the room where the dead girl laid. Perhaps as they entered, the girl did, in fact, look as if she were simply sleeping.

Jairus saw, then, the corpse of his little girl for the first time. We might imagine his face twisting in grief as the reality set in. They had been unable to alleviate her suffering. Now there was

---

8. I've met a lot of people who offer misery for free these days.

nothing they could do. The only thing left to hope for was the possibility that this timely visitor would change everything, but they had little reason to expect a miracle except Jesus' strange words.

Jesus took the girl by the hand, again violating the ceremonial law by touching a dead body. Elder of the synagogue or not, Jairus probably didn't care anymore. The disciples and girl's parents held their collective breath, and Jesus said, "Talitha cumi" ("little girl, I say to you, arise").

Just like the scene at Nain, Jesus commanded this specific individual to get up.

As soon as he spoke, the girl stood and began moving around the room. The witnesses of the event were quick to point out that she didn't need to rebuild her strength or come to, as if she'd been in a coma. She is immediately *resuscitated* and *whole*. Luke says her spirit returned at once, which I think is an important distinction to make. The girl's spirit returned to the same body, not a new or resurrected one. The daughter of Jairus had come back from the dead.

TWO STRANGE COMMANDS

This tale comes to a bit of a strange conclusion. Jesus performed one of the greatest recorded acts in all of human history and then issued two commands as specific as they are bizarre. First, as the family embraced and the disciples looked on slack jawed, Jesus instructed them not to tell anyone about what had just happened.

Don't tell anyone? That's an odd thing to say to a family who just experienced the death and rebirth of a child in one day. Later Jesus told his disciples to go into all the world and teach about his commands. Why would the same man who seems to advocate world evangelism tell these folks not to tell a soul?

This isn't the only time Jesus does this. Mark 1 tells the story of Jesus healing a man with leprosy, and after the miracle, Jesus said, "See that you don't tell this to anyone." Who can blame the cured man for dropping the ball on that one? "Instead he went out and began to talk freely, spreading the news. As a result, Jesus could no longer enter a town openly but stayed outside in lonely places." Perhaps there is our answer for why Jesus wanted to keep things under wraps.

Of course, the story of Jairus and his daughter was eventually told. Matthew says that people all over the region heard, and the tale is still amazing audiences two thousand years later. Jesus didn't mean that those witnesses were never to speak of what they had seen ever again, just not at that time. Imagine how these people would've told the stories throughout their lives to family members and friends. They would've told their children and grandchildren, and I wonder when that all ended. How many generations until those stories were forgotten? You might think someone delusional if they told you that your great-great-great grandma had been raised from the dead.

So we're left with a written record and nothing more. We have to use our imaginations to fill in some parts of the story's epilogue. I wonder what those mourners thought when they saw the little girl walking around. After all, Jesus did tell them she was merely sleeping before kicking them out of the house. They had been laughing at him only minutes before and were as certain that the girl had died as that guy in the ambulance was that he was sitting next to a wounded cop and not his worst nightmare wearing someone else's face. But Jesus wasn't joking. To God, this story seems to be telling us, death truly is temporary. Bodies die and decay, but our souls, who we are, never cease to exist.

Jesus' second strange command was to give the girl something to eat. He just raised her from the dead yet left her with an empty stomach? Like the instruction to keep quiet about what had happened in that room, Jesus again acts in a way that doesn't make a whole lot of sense at first glance.

"Make sure you feed her," he said. There's beauty in that simple statement. He's concerned about those things we need but so often forget. The Scriptures say that God is the bread of life, after all. God not only takes care of our greatest needs but also tends to the simplest parts of our lives.

HEAVEN AND EGG ROLLS

My friend Ellie says that food is very spiritual. Maybe that's why everyone says her egg rolls are divine. I've never had one of her egg rolls, so I wouldn't know how good they are, but I think about them enough to get distracted when I'm trying to write. Ellie says that eating together bonds us the same as Jesus and the disciples at the Last Supper or the great feasts that the Bible says will happen in heaven. I bet I'll have egg rolls when I'm in heaven.

Ellie told me that the Old Testament prophet Elijah got very depressed. You would think that he would be a little happier since God let him do cool stuff like raise people from the dead, but Elijah got depressed. And God sent him food to make him feel better.

I told Ellie that it was weird how Jesus wanted Jairus and his wife to feed their daughter immediately after she was raised from the dead, but she thought it made a lot of sense.

"This little family gets to eat together, and Jesus would be there, and they'd be laughing together. When a friend comes to you and they are down and depressed, you take them to get coffee and eat some warm cookies together. Do you know what I mean?"

"Huh?" I was thinking about warm cookies.

We were talking on the phone, but I'm pretty sure she rolled her eyes at me. "Everybody brings food to a funeral because it's comforting. What could be more refreshing to someone who feels dead than to eat good food with people you love? When we eat good food together we feel better."

"That's true," I said, trying to open a bag of cookies without her hearing.

"When you see a person who's spiritually dead then just feed them! Anybody can do that."

I think Ellie's right. It's probably why people connect chicken soup and the soul. Perhaps we think we need to do amazing things for people when they are hurting, but really we just need to give them a warm cookie or something. Feeding someone in need is a great start in the quest for spiritual meaning and life.

NEVER TOO LATE

I really believe that God will be there for us no matter how far gone we are, that he is pursuing us and will never stop chasing after us. The key is in how we respond. Jairus went for Jesus, found him, and waited on him.

Sometimes we feel the weight of something in our lives that is completely beyond our control. We may feel like a spiritual zombie—sluggish, shambling without direction, loaded down by the baggage of our lives. Life can paralyze us, but I believe no matter what we go through we are not forgotten and can have a miraculous meeting with the God of the universe just like Jairus did on that humid shore. We may wait amid a sea of people, but I believe he sees us and actually *wants* to do something incredible in our lives.

We miss out on life-changing opportunities for a number of reasons. Many of us can probably relate to Jairus who had to overcome pride and set aside his standing in that community in order to ask for help. He had stood with friends and colleagues who were opposed to Jesus in the weeks and months prior to his daughter's sickness. We don't know if he had ever felt contempt for Jesus like so many of the religious leaders, but a transformation definitely took place within him.

It's striking that the powerful synagogue ruler and the shunned bleeding woman both ended up on the dirty ground before Jesus. Mark says, "Then the woman, knowing what had happened to her, came and fell at his feet" (Mark 5:33). She was as disregarded as Jairus was respected, yet they were both humbly approaching their only hope for healing. The bleeding woman didn't understand how exactly it worked, but she knew that she had been healed.

Pain is precisely the reason why many of us decide to reject God or even the idea of God. Suffering is a part of life, and so each of us has to decide if God causes it with malice or cares for us in spite of it. I do know that when pain gets bad enough you can actually go numb and become empty inside like a zombie. We all have to find our way out of spiritual and emotional tombs from time to time. Most people never make it out once they're dead and buried—except a man named Lazarus.

CHAPTER 5

THE FRIEND

Call no man happy until he is dead.

—Aeschylus

The thirty-three-year-old man was dead, no doubt about it. He had no pulse. His body was taken away to be prepared for burial, and the medical examiners placed him on a table to begin the autopsy. Their first incision was on the man's face, but as they cut, he began to bleed. Something was wrong. Dead men don't bleed. Just as that thought started to form in the doctor's mind, chaos ensued: the supposedly dead man awoke in terror, flailing and screaming.

It seemed that someone made a terrible mistake that day in 2007 by declaring Carlos Camejo dead after a traffic accident in Venezuela, but he was a victim (or fortunate recipient) of a rare

71

phenomenon in which people can autoresuscitate after being declared dead.

Camejo said the pain of the procedure woke him up. Unbearable, he called it. I bet!

The condition that allowed Camejo to return to life is known as Lazarus Syndrome, a mysterious occurrence that's only been recorded about three dozen times. This medical anomaly is named for the New Testament Lazarus who was brought back to life by Jesus after spending four days in a tomb in which he was very much dead.

Ask someone to list people who were raised from the dead in the Bible and Lazarus is often the first name to come up. A lot of folks have learned the basics of the event, particularly churchgoers. During Sunday school back in the day we even had flannelgraphs—storyboards covered with flannel. Teachers stuck cutouts of characters and objects on the board to jazz up stories.[1] You had "dead Lazarus" as well as "back-to-life Lazarus," for example. I think I heard the story so much while growing up that I never fully stopped to consider how amazing something like that would be.

CONFUSED BY JESUS

Jesus was a guy who loved meeting people and hanging out with friends. We often miss that part of his story. It's easy to focus

---

1. Eventually computers and PowerPoint came along, so churches released their stronghold on flannel and Gen Xers like me started wearing it all the time.

on his life as it's told in the Gospels and not consider a fuller picture of his experiences—he kept busy and worked hard. People constantly demanded his attention or action in their lives, so he enjoyed kicking back for a nice meal someone had prepared. I'm sure he could cut loose, tell stories, and belly laugh with the best of them.

Two of Jesus' good friends were sisters named Mary and Martha. They offered him rest and a good meal when he and the disciples were in town. He knew the family well and stayed with them on multiple occasions. Jesus also cared about their brother Lazarus, who became ill (John 11). The sisters knew what Jesus was able to do, so they sent word for him to hurry to them. That's when the one they loved, a man they called Lord, did nothing. Jesus told everyone that Lazarus's sickness wasn't going to lead to death and that God would be glorified. Then they stayed put for two more days.

In the meantime, Lazarus succumbed to sickness and died. Martha and Mary watched their brother fight, hope, suffer, and then die. They called for Jesus, but he didn't come. The people in Bethany were beside themselves wondering why Jesus didn't understand the significance of the situation. The sisters didn't understand why Jesus hadn't shown up when they needed him so desperately.

STUCK IN A TOMB

Here are the basics of what we know about Lazarus in this story. He knew Jesus, he got sick, he died, and he had been in the tomb for *four days* by the time Jesus finally arrived.

That tomb. You might not think that the most relatable person in this story is Lazarus, but the literal death of Lazarus can be a metaphor for the spiritual death so many of us experience. We've talked about this already in previous chapters: we go through painful experiences and spiritual sickness; we even end up in different kinds of tombs where we become trapped in a dark place of mental and spiritual decay.

Our emotional tombs can be made out of a number of things. Many of the problems that paralyze us are rooted in anxiety—worrying about things beyond our control. We still worry, even though it changes nothing. When it gets bad enough, anxiety can cause insomnia and even turn a bed into a virtual tomb as you lie there through the dark night, eyes open into nothingness as your thoughts race and your heart pounds. The claustrophobia of a tomb can represent worry.

Sometimes we are trapped by anger. Unresolved issues build into the distraction of resentment, and left unchecked, those feelings can spiral out of control and create explosive moments of blind rage. The entrapment of a tomb can represent anger too.

Another powerful force is depression, that silent spiritual killer lingering in the darkest corners of our minds. Depression robs us of more than motivation; time itself disappears, especially as unconsciousness becomes preferable to waking existence. When life is so painful that you can't even function, the very act of breathing, let alone eating, becomes challenging. The complete darkness of a tomb mirrors depression.

We lose control when we're in emotional tombs, and forces

that we can't handle take over. We long to fix the problems on our own, but those efforts usually turn out badly—at least in my experience, they do.

Spiritual tombs come in many varieties as well. A lot of problems begin with confusion when we don't understand God's action—or inaction—in the world. He just doesn't make sense, and we start to wonder what's going on. That's when we are likely to make decisions that turn out poorly even though they made sense in our minds. Get enough confusion pent up in your head, and doubt is never far behind. The spiritual tomb of doubt is closely related to feeling distanced from God. Questions fill dark, doubt-filled crypts. Is God really out there? Does he really care about me? Can I trust him?

Temptation is another spiritual killer. We can all become trapped by vices that grip deep into our hearts. Whether a physical need, mental longing, or attitude of the heart, we all struggle with recurring temptation.

Life circumstances also weigh upon us. Some people become trapped in bad situations. Relationships, jobs, and destructive patterns keep many of us entombed. And often we don't choose to escape these tombs; instead, we somehow find safety in these places, as if we're saying, "This place isn't pleasant, but at least nothing else can hurt me, and I can kind of manage what I'm up against if it's familiar enough." The possibility of success is often more frightening than the familiarity of failure. We fear the unknown and entomb ourselves.

We have to be honest about the struggles we all face if we ever hope to escape these tombs of life. We may be in denial, but God is not. He's aware of our situation. It's not some complicated struggle to God that needs to be figured out. There's no guarantee of instant happiness or pain-free living, but life can get better. It may be tough as we battle our demons, but God wants to get us out of our emotional and spiritual tombs. And, as Lazarus discovered, God can do it.

WE ARE OUT OF CONTROL

If you were to pitch the story of Lazarus to a Hollywood studio, you could package the movie as a race against time. Instead of needing some mysterious potion in a medicine vial, Martha knew the only cure for her brother was the miraculous power of God. They dispatched the messengers to Jesus, and if you do the math in this story, they reached him just in time—on the day Lazarus died. But Jesus didn't race to the scene of Lazarus's deathbed for a last-minute save like he did for Jairus. In fact, Jesus didn't act at all, even though the individuals involved in this story knew that he had the power to heal people from long-distance. He had done exactly that for the daughter of a Roman military commander (Luke 7:1-10). A Roman! One of the bad guys. And now Jesus couldn't even say a word to help his friend Lazarus whom he supposedly loved?

Jesus arrived in town four days *after* the burial. Martha went straight out to meet him and said, "Lord, if you had been here, my brother would not have died" (John 11:32).

Poor Martha was in a tomb herself of sadness and confusion and pain. She liked to take and be in control, yet she couldn't get a handle on any part of this tragedy. She couldn't fix her brother or manage the situation. Everything she feared most was happening, and she didn't know what to do. But even though she questioned Jesus, she quickly followed up with a statement of pure faith. "But even now I know that God will give you whatever you ask" (John 11:22 NLT).

Mixed emotions were already beginning to stir within Jesus as Martha spoke. He told her that Lazarus would rise again, but she thought he was referring to the end of time when everyone would be resurrected as they commonly believed at the time. That's when Jesus dropped one of the biggest statements in history on her:

"I am the resurrection and the life. Those who believe in me, even though they die like everyone else, will live again. They are given eternal life for believing in me and will never perish. Do you believe this?" (v. 25 NLT).

Martha said, "Yes, Lord. I have always believed you are the Messiah, the Son of God, the one who has come into the world from God" (v. 27 NLT).

Martha's response makes me think that belief might be the most beautiful thing we can see amid brokenness. But all was not right in Bethany. Someone was missing. Mary had not come out to see her beloved Jesus. She was still inside.

WHERE WAS GOD?

As soon as Mary heard that Jesus was in town and asking for her, she got up, quickly went to meet him, and fell at his feet. Her statement to him has echoed throughout the centuries: "Lord, if you had been here . . ." It's probably not a coincidence that each sister said the exact same thing to Jesus. They had probably said something like that to each other a few times in the days since their brother died.

John 11:33 describes Jesus' reaction: "Therefore, when Jesus saw her weeping, and the Jews who came with her weeping, He groaned in the spirit and was troubled" (NKJV).

Biblical scholar A. T. Robertson once described this word *groan* as meaning "to snort with anger like a horse." Can you imagine Jesus huffing in exasperation? The scene demonstrates the extent of his humanity. He's not happy about the situation. One of his friends is dead, and the rest are either heartbroken or missing the point. On top of all that, he's back in enemy territory. As John describes the moment, Jesus gets disturbed as Mary weeps and *the other Jews follow her.* He called for Mary, not an entire crowd, but they followed her anyway and intruded on the privacy of this tough moment, especially with their loud mourning. You can bet that Jesus didn't appreciate big shows of disingenuous emotion that weren't heartfelt.[2] Some of these followers might also have been around when the crowd tried to kill Jesus just weeks earlier. He maintains self-control despite all the frustration, but he's clearly not happy. That angry grunt had to be pretty intimidating.

I can relate to Mary's question: "Where were you, God?" It's hard not to throw an accusatory tone his way when things go wrong. We often struggle with all the horrible things that happen,

---

2. For what it's worth, people who act like that today are still annoying.

especially to innocent people. Millions have asked why bad things happen to good people. I think that's just an extension of asking, "Why is this happening to *me*?"

The timing doesn't always make sense, and we may not understand why tragedies are allowed to take place in our lives, but the story of Lazarus demonstrates some important realities. One being that God is deeply moved by what we say and do. When something terrible happens it's easy to say that if God really loved us then he wouldn't have let such disaster into our lives. But according to this story he loved Lazarus and still didn't stop the tragedy of his friend's death.

I wonder what it's like to hear prayers like God does. I remember one time in eighth grade when a classmate wanted to pray for the Pittsburgh Penguins because they were in the Stanley Cup Finals against the Minnesota North Stars. I remember wondering if any kids in Minnesota were praying and how God would feel about them.[3] That's a silly example, but consider the Civil War in America, during which hundreds of thousands of people prayed that God would grant them victory. The North and South wanted completely different things, yet people from both sides loved and appealed to God.

We have no idea how this all works and so our choice is to decide whether or not to trust God. People who are way smarter than I am offer examples of how God uses pain and suffering for our good, and though sometimes those examples are comforting,

---

3. Apparently God liked Pittsburgh better because the Penguins won the series in six games.

mostly pain just sucks. The bottom line is that we don't get the full picture because we're not God. A challenging key to spiritual life is being OK with that.

Finally, they led Jesus to the tomb of his friend, and the shortest verse in the Bible tells us that he wept. Jesus knew that even death was curable but still hated to see Mary's sadness amid the tangible effects of sin and death. In the midst of confusion and pain I find it comforting to think that God sees us, hears us, and weeps with us.

COME FORTH!

Anyone who grew up around Christian pop culture of the 1980s and 1990s remembers Carman. If you know who that is then the simple mention of his name sums up a lot. If you've never heard of Carman, try to imagine a curly-haired, white, Italian, Pentecostal rapper. Maybe you just had to be there, but the guy used to put on a wild show with theatrics and dancing, and it just sounds even more bizarre the more I try to explain it.

My first memory of Carman was of his famous song in which he plays the speaking part of Lazarus who suddenly finds himself in heaven for a bit. Lazarus is having a blast, chatting it up with ancestral heroes like Samson, Moses, and David when he suddenly hears a familiar voice calling out his name.

Of course, back here on earth Lazarus wasn't doing so well. We're talking about a guy in a tomb in the Mediterranean climate for four days. If you're wondering what that might look like, try tossing a turkey, organs and all, in the oven on 100-plus degrees for four days. So you can understand the reactions when Jesus told the bystanders to move the large stone away from the tomb. Despite her faith just minutes earlier, even Martha had some grave misgivings. I love the way the King James Version puts it: "He stinketh."

Jesus once again groans, disturbed by the whole scene around him. As the stone is levered out of the way he prays out loud to be sure everyone around knows why he's doing what he's doing: to demonstrate the power of God. Then he raises his voice for those three powerful words: "Lazarus, come out!"

Jesus told Martha that he was the resurrection and the life and claimed power over death. Notice that each time he raises someone from the dead he speaks specifically to them. I like to think that with that kind of power, if he would have simply said "Rise!" or "Come forth!" then every dead person in earshot might have shown up. So he specifically called each one by name. To the widow's son he said, "Young man." To the daughter of Jairus he said, "Little girl." And to his own friend he said, "Lazarus, come forth!"

In each case his call is personal.

Everybody gawks at the dark entrance to the tomb. The mummy is about to come out. In movies I always yell at stupid characters who stand there and watch as the creature slowly emerges from the grave to kill them. Why wouldn't you run? There's a scene like this in the 1979 movie *Zombie*, which is considered a classic by people who love such things. It also features a zombie eating a shark, and I'm fairly certain that's never happened again. These people end up on a zombie-infested island in the Caribbean where naturally their vehicle breaks down, so they head into the jungle on foot where they discover an old burial ground filled with the bodies of Spanish conquistadors. Just your typical weekend really. Mayhem ensues as decaying Spaniards start crawling out of their graves. There's this scene during which one of the ladies sees a dead guy rising out of his grave, and it must take a half hour for this creature to finally stand up and move toward her. All the while she's screaming her head off like an idiot. Does she do something logical or useful like run away? Of course not. She stands there screaming until her untimely death, which, let's be honest, you're kind of rooting for at that point. I don't know, maybe it is more realistic to be paralyzed with fear in the face of something as shocking as a dead man walking out of his grave. At the very least I suppose disbelief is to be expected.

I'm trying to wrap my brain around the scene at the tomb of Lazarus, one of the most amazing stories ever told, and John describes the moment in almost comically understated terms: "The dead man came out."

Oh, that's all?

At least he didn't start eating everybody.

Wrapped in linen from head to foot, Lazarus must have been kind of hopping along, dust and rocks kicking up as he emerged from the darkness of the cave. But the decay everyone expected was gone. His internal organs were even up and running. Everyone was in shock. Everyone except Jesus who said, "Take off the grave clothes and let him go."

I can't imagine what it would be like to witness something so incredible. But then he says to get in there and physically remove the burial linens. First off, that's gross. Bugs, worms, and stuff. Second, our instincts usually tell us to move *away* from walking corpses. You should not only get away from walking corpses but do so fast. Referring back to Columbus from *Zombieland*, rule #1 is cardio. As he says, "Zombies lead a very active lifestyle. So should you." Dead people waking up and walking around had to be just as freaky in the first century as it is in the twenty-first century. Third, Jewish custom is still anti-corpse touching. Jesus shocked a lot of folks when he touched those other dead people, but now he has *others* touching a corpse!

Then again, is it technically still a corpse once it walks out of the grave?

Notice that Jesus doesn't just blast the stone away from the tomb with his mind or produce a squeaky clean Lazarus. He tells the people counting on him that *they* have to move the heavy stone and remove the nasty grave clothes. For these people, encountering the power of God was a personal thing, not always neat and tidy. Jesus expected them to get involved and do something.

For us, it is also true. We can't make a difference in this world without committing to the lives of others, but commitment is never easy. A lot of us talk like we want to change the world but a single life right in front of us is much more real and more difficult. We say we want to make a difference but often hesitate. Perhaps the task seems too difficult—or stinky.

We might believe that God's purposes for us are good, but when it comes down to it we are often more comfortable staying in our tombs than stepping into the light where we can find healing and meaning. Imagine the story going like this:

Jesus: "Lazarus, come out!"

Lazarus: "Huh? Uh, no thanks, Jesus. I'm good in here. Appreciate you stopping by, though."

Yet that's exactly what we do sometimes: choose death over life.

JESUS ISN'T SAFE

Jesus didn't play it safe or use generic language to teach hollow platitudes. He had an edge because he lived on the edge. He shook things up and called people out for their hypocrisy and corruption regardless of their social standing.

After his reappearing act with Lazarus, the crowd went wild, but they were sharply divided. Many of them put their faith in Jesus, but some ran off like tattletales to the Pharisees who were so blinded by greed for their own power that they missed everything. Their collective reaction was a big "Oh no he didn't!" and from that day on they plotted to kill him.

Jesus and the disciples retreated to a quiet village as Jerusalem began filling with many visitors arriving for Jewish Passover. Instead of preparing to worship God, the chief priests and Pharisees used the temple as headquarters for their sting operation to trap Jesus if he decided to show up once more. Just six days before Passover, Jesus returned to Bethany for a celebration dinner in his honor at the home of a man named Simon the Leper. Martha served as hostess as Lazarus kicked back with his friend who brought him back to life. After a while the guests who had gathered began to smell something, a powerful fragrance of perfume. Mary was back at the feet of Jesus, this time in complete reverence. She poured out an expensive bottle of perfume worth an entire year's wages and used it to wipe his feet with her hair. What better way to bury the memory of that smell of death than with the fragrance of worship.

Before long, word spread around town that Jesus was back, and he was at Simon's house with new local celebrity Lazarus. Everyone was talking about those two and a large crowd followed. The religious leaders saw how many people were dedicated to Jesus because of Lazarus, the walking miracle. That did it. They expanded their murderous plot with plans to kill him as well. The religious leaders wanted to put Lazarus to death because he was a threat.

The fact that Lazarus was targeted like that seems a little harsh. You would think that dying would be the hard part, but life doesn't necessarily get easy after you come back from the dead.

It's tempting to want it to be easy, though. You can pick out all the good parts of the Bible to make it look like we just need to give God a cosmic thumbs up and we'll be blessed with happiness and riches. That's a really nice thought, that if we just believe in God we'll all be healthy and wealthy, but this story is filled with people whom God loved yet they still went through sickness, gut-wrenching anxiety, and death. The disciples traveling with Jesus were prepared to face persecution and even death just for associating with him. And the religious leaders wanted to put Lazarus to death because he was living proof of the divine nature of Jesus.

Believing in God doesn't guarantee happiness, prosperity, or even great hair days.[4] This might seem too harsh, but I'm not sure what could possibly offer this. Is there some alternative that provides nothing but truth, prosperity, and happiness?

Mary and Martha felt let down by Jesus. He didn't come through in the way they expected. He didn't do what they believed he would. Yet they still ended up back in his loving embrace. I love picturing all those who physically clutched Jesus. As they embraced him and laid their head against his chest, they heard his heart beating. They literally heard and felt the heartbeat of God. Life happens to us all, good and bad alike. Jesus knew as much when he said that "In this world you will have trouble. But take heart! I have overcome the world" (John 16:33).

DO YOU WANT TO GET WELL?

It's interesting to note the progression of the three recorded accounts in which Jesus raised someone from the dead. In the first case, with the widow at Nain, he went to her. We're not told if the

---

4. The hairstyles of televangelists over the past few decades kind of proves this.

woman had any idea who Jesus was or not when he showed up at her son's funeral. In the second instance, Jairus knew of Jesus and sought him out. We see a desperate individual pursuing a known miracle worker. Now in this third event we see people who personally know Jesus making an urgent plea. Moreover, John points out that Jesus' love for his ailing friend Lazarus was evident.

God addresses each person's situation regardless of their social status, gender, economic situation, or anything else. God's response doesn't always make sense, but the Bible holds no record of God ever disregarding a heartfelt plea.

The man who woke up during his own autopsy helps me believe that no one is irredeemable to God. Medical science still can't explain modern miracles in which people die and somehow return to life. One doctor wrote, "A case of Lazarus syndrome . . . is a humbling reminder to find that our efforts and judgements are not necessarily the final arbiters of outcome. Perhaps it is a supreme hubris on our part to presume that we can reliably distinguish the reversible from the irreversible, or the salvageable from the nonsalvageable."[5]

What is irreversible to God? I believe that every life is salvageable. The simple yet exhilarating truth is that we can be transformed. Simple isn't necessarily easy, and the process of changing is usually tough since new beginnings carry both promise and pain. Birth isn't easy; why should rebirth be any more so?

5. Bruce Ben-David et al., *Survival After Failed Intraoperative Resuscitation: A Case of "Lazarus Syndrome,"* Anesthesia & Analgesia 92.3 (2001): 690–92.

You can't go around raising people from the dead without making a splash, and Jesus attracted enemies as well as admirers. Ironically, he moved one step closer to his own death each time he brought somebody back to life. When he walked up to the tomb of his friend Lazarus and brought the dead man back to life, he enraged his enemies. His crucifixion followed extremely high-profile events in which dead people came back to life. The enemies of Jesus did not discount his ability to raise the dead. Maybe we shouldn't either. After all, we are fairly obsessed with death.

CHAPTER 6

THE PLACES OF DEATH

If you wanna live life on your own terms gotta be willing to crash and burn.

—Vince Neil

We've spent a few chapters looking at life-giving miracles. Our historical records describe three specific instances in which Jesus brought someone back from the dead in the first century. We know where each of those characters was brought back to life—during a funeral, in a house, at a tomb—but we don't know where or how they died. I mentioned earlier that although death isn't our favorite topic, we still learn a lot through it during our lives. Put simply, life is a gift that we cherish more and more as we age and learn more about the reality of dying.

Spiritual life is also a gift. Inner peace and contentment is magical, and we all want that kind of fulfillment in our lives. Memories of good times when our world seemed right are happy things to ponder. Like Lazarus, Jairus, and the people of Nain, we never forget the details about where we were when something changed our lives for the better.

We don't like to think about the opposite side of that coin—the places that symbolize our failures—but we should. Some of us do nothing but focus on our shortcomings and every mistake we've ever made, spending every second waiting for something to go wrong so that when it does we can say, "See!" But that's not healthy behavior. On the other hand, some of us prefer to hang out in la-la land where nothing bad ever happens and delicious fruit candies grow on trees.[1] That never works either because an unresolved past is like a zombie—you can try to bury it, but it's still not dead and may come back to bite you at any moment.

We have to figure out how to effectively deal with our past in order to truly put it down once and for all and to never have to fear being buried by it again. I'd like to take a few pages to think about those places of struggle, where we are challenged and sometimes even come face-to-face with the meaning of death in our lives.

---

1. OK, I made that last part up. Everyone knows that Skittles don't grow on trees, not even in la-la land.

WHEN YOU LEAST EXPECT IT

I never thought I would see anybody die at work. I'm a college teacher, so it's not like I'm a doctor or a cop or anything. But on student survey day, I found myself in a life-and-death situation.

We administer surveys of student opinions one day out of every semester. On these days, I have to stop lecturing fifteen minutes early and leave the room so students won't be embarrassed when they write all about how I'm the greatest professor they've ever had or something. It was because of this uncommon event on this particular day that I walked out of my classroom early and into an almost empty hallway.

With my bag slung over my shoulder, I closed the door behind me. That's when I heard a coworker calling for help and pointing at a fellow teacher standing frozen at the door to his office. I didn't understand what was happening at first, but I dropped my bag and ran to where he was. I thought his hand was stuck in the door but as I reached him I realized the situation was much worse.

He couldn't move. I half-carried him into his office and got him into a chair, and because of the way I was positioned I ended up kneeling with this stricken man in a sort of half hug. There was commotion and some panic around us as we waited for emergency medical responders.

The man was unable to verbalize anything, so I asked the colleague who called for help what his name was. I tried to communicate with him, but nothing worked. His eyes were open with awareness, but his body was betraying him. He squeezed at my shoulder as his only form of communication. Then his eyes went wide and distant. His face paled and his skin chilled. I grabbed his face in both my palms and called for him, tried to bring him back to focus. I steadied his head from rolling and heard gasps behind me. I didn't know what to do. He wore a bracelet with a saint on it, Simon or Jude I think, and I whispered prayers for him that I hoped he could hear.

He never recovered. The medics arrived and rushed him to the hospital, but he succumbed that evening. What at first had seemed to be strokelike symptoms were actually a powerful heart attack.

I did a lot of thinking about life and death after that. I thought about the man who lived so many decades, had so many experiences, yet he spent some of his final moments in the arms of a person he had never met.

When you watch someone die you suddenly realize how very much alive you are.

CLOUDS OF BREATH, VISIONS OF DEATH

I live in Pittsburgh where the winters get cold. I won't say it can get really cold because then my friends in Canada will make fun of me. But we have plenty of winter days where our breath turns into big poofs of airborne heat, and a lot of people complain on those days. They don't like cold weather. (They also complain when it's too hot, but that's another story.) I try to thank God for the very fact that I'm alive, that I have a working body with hands to write and a voice to speak.

Watching my coworker fade from this life challenged my perspective about freezing cold days. I realized that every single breath I take is made and granted by God. When I see those white poofs of my life force crashing into the cold, now I see a miracle. Those breaths are all that separate me from eternity.

I've been thinking about where I'll likely die someday and figure it will probably be Pittsburgh because that's where I've done most of my living. But that's a silly expectation. You usually can't plan these things. I could just as easily die in Canada where it's really cold.

Speaking of really cold places, there's a story set in Barrow, Alaska, called *30 Days of Night*. The comic book miniseries-turned-movie tells the story of some feisty vampires who go to Barrow where they can enjoy thirty straight days of darkness as a result of the region's geographic uniqueness. It's a blood-sucking Mardi Gras, and a good time was sure to be had by all until the vampire leader finds out what those punk vampire kids are doing. Can't have the whole world finding out you exist, he says, and heads north to show them who's who (or at least what's what). Meanwhile, the sheriff of Barrow can't have vampires eating all his townies, so he takes the last option available and injects himself with vampire blood in order to get super strong and kill the head vampire. No sooner does he take care of business than he learns that the extreme weather makes being a creature of the night anything but fun in Barrow.

The sun is finally set to rise again right about the time the sheriff is hating life as a vampire. Weakened and tragic, he decides to take in the sunrise with his girl even though it's guaranteed to kill him and leave her hugging a big blanket full of ashes. He goes out on his own terms though. But the point is that going out on any terms, yours or someone else's, is still going out.

BRUSHES WITH DEATH

I came really close to dying once. My best friend Dave and I were seniors in high school going to visit my sister at her house. We pulled onto a highway and were broadsided by a car going at least sixty miles per hour. Dave hit the gas pedal at the last second, and instead of a direct impact we were sent spinning in a violent collision that exploded every tire and window on the car. I wasn't wearing a seatbelt (for the last time) and was thrown into the backseat.

I don't think I was out for long, but the next thing I knew a man was putting fingers in my face and asking me to count them. Everything had gone into slow motion, and sound disappeared for a short time. The glass in my mouth reminded me of sand after getting rolled by a wave at the beach. Dave was slumped over the steering wheel, and I was afraid he was dead.

We both walked away.

When I was in grad school, I was at a friend's house one night with a bunch of buddies. The night seemed normal as ever, but as I walked out of the bathroom, this overwhelming sensation fell over me. I was alone, upstairs, and could hear laughter downstairs as I slowly leaned against the kitchen wall and slid down into a heap.

I distinctly remember thinking that my life was ending as I stared up at the ceiling and passed out. I had strayed far from the path God hopes for us, and for a brief moment, I thought God must be really disappointed in me, dying in a kitchen like that.

I'm convinced we all think about God as we die, regardless of whether or not we spend our lives focusing on a higher power. There is clarity in death; I've seen it in people as they've died. I saw it on the face of my poor colleague that day as I knelt beside him, and he looked far beyond me, beyond this physical world.

I once heard a young man recount his suicide attempt. As a teenager, he leaped from the Golden Gate Bridge in San Francisco. Miraculously, he lived to tell his story and caution other young people that life was worth living. He said that as soon as his feet left the ledge, an unbearable terror exploded in him, a realization that he had made a horrific mistake. He said he felt like he was falling into hell even though he had never thought about anything like that before. He believed that God was real and had saved him. He found meaning in midair.

During that sudden car accident, I didn't have a second to process my impending death. But as I slid down that wall in my friend's house, thinking I was dying, I had a moment to think. And I felt like my life had been such a waste. I wanted to apologize to God for spending my life so selfishly, always trying to make myself happy and win the approval of others. I wondered how I could know so much truth and yet care so little about it.

Of course, I didn't die. I regained consciousness and went back downstairs before anyone realized what had happened. Even though I was alive, healthy, and in my prime, I was spiritually dead on the inside. My existence was a Seinfeld episode, a life about nothing. I secretly wondered if God was done with warning shots and would take me out for real the next time. It may sound crazy, but I constantly felt like I was in the Creator's sights. That's a terrible way to live: completely guilt-ridden, wondering how long you'll be allowed to continue your fraudulent existence.

OUT OF BOUNDS

Physically, we can die anywhere, but spiritually, most of us die outside the lines. A pastor friend of mine named Mike introduced this concept. We became friends a couple years back as I was going through some major life changes, my own personal apocalypse you could say. You've probably experienced an earth-shattering event or two yourself. Sometimes people die, relationships end, we screw up big, or any number of other personal disasters befall us. It was right around a time like that when Mike told me I was like one of the greatest quarterbacks in the world.

"I don't play football," I said.

"That's not what I mean, Clay. A quarterback can step onto the field and do what maybe only four or five other people on the planet are capable of, but what good is that if he can't handle himself *off* the field?"

He would make a ton of money and be filthy rich, I thought, but knew this wasn't what he wanted to hear.

Mike continued. "He could be the most gifted player in the world but will lose the privilege to even compete if he can't keep it together in his personal life."

"Okay, so what does this have to do with me?"

"Guys like you and me are gifted in a way that puts us in front of people, but there's a lot of responsibility that comes with that. You might be able to stand in front of people and give a great talk, but you've got to be just as good *outside* the lines, in your personal life."

He was right. And this had been my downfall. I feared that the proper word to describe such a problem was *hypocrisy,* one of the worst forms of spiritual death in which we don't even realize how sick we are.

At the same time, Pastor Mike—a different Pastor Mike, actually—told me how people looked up to me and how I speak with great authority. I thought he was being very kind.

Then he said this: "But that's not who you really are."

Hello, dagger. At the time, I had been slowly waking from my spiritual death, but his words were like defibrillator paddles shocking me back to life. He was dead on.

I guess the moral of the story is beware of pastors named Mike. Kidding. I know those guys really care about me because they told me the truth in love. Those conversations were real turning points for me. I didn't want to be different on the inside than I appeared on the outside.

It's easy to point the finger when people screw up in really high-profile ways, but most of us will die on the sidelines, out of sight of the world's watchful eye. The sidelines have looked different at various points in my life—cars with my friends during high school, dark kitchens during college, even living rooms full of family. The sidelines represent personal life.

We don't want to be like vampires, hiding away in a cold, dark crypt anytime the light of the world shines on us. That's the kind of thinking that turns God into Santa Claus, making a list of naughty and nice, eager to send us coal for the slightest infraction. God's not like that.

THE LONELIEST CROWD AT CHRISTMAS

A cemetery is a strange place to be on Christmas, when most of us celebrate the holidays with festive traditions. Depending on where you live, a blanket of snow or sunshine or leaves may cover the ground, but the rest is pretty much the same everywhere: neat rows of headstones of varying heights.

Christmas heightens sentimentality, especially when we've lost a loved one. We count the years since we last celebrated with him or her. Many of us go to the cemetery every year around Christmas to ensure that the grave marker of our loved one commemorates the season in some way. I've seen holiday wreaths, red bows, vigil lights, even multicolored tinsel.

Last year I drove deep into a cemetery on Christmas Day. The afternoon light dimmed as a captivating sunset over the mountainous horizon to the west painted the gray sky with a pinkish orange that faded into purple. It was bright and beautiful to look at even from a place where death surrounded me. I leaned against an ancient maple tree. Its massive roots drove into the soft Pennsylvania soil like anchor chains. Standing on the knots of those roots, I wondered how far down they went. I watched the sky while a lonely squirrel squeaked somewhere nearby in the soft breeze, thinking the spot wouldn't be such a bad place to be laid for eternal rest. It was really quite beautiful, that place of death. As the sun faded, the orange sky dipped below the mountains like a fading fire. It got cold, and I moved on.

I walked around, looking at the stones. I read the names and dates of resting souls and, like one of Dickens's ghosts, thought about all the Christmases they had celebrated. I imagined some of the experiences they might have had during their lifetimes. I saw the grave of a woman who lived in the 1950s and wondered if she preferred Bing Crosby or Elvis. Another marker documented a young man born in 1900 who lived just eighteen short years. Had the great flu epidemic taken his life? Would he have gone off to World War I in Europe had he lived? What had he thought when news of the Titanic sinking reached his small corner of Pennsylvania?

Cemeteries fascinate me. I'm intrigued because the people remembered there have no idea what the world turned into, but I have no idea about their experience beyond this life. They have glimpsed what only the departed can glimpse. As I look at the markers of these lives I consider the past as well as the future. Where were they back then? Where are they now? What did people say at their funerals? What will people say at mine?

There are thousands of stories buried in every cemetery, most of them blending into the forgotten background of history. There could be something unsettling or even frightening in that thought, but I also find a lot of inspiration in it. About three thousand years ago David considered the vastness of the universe and asked "What is man that you are mindful of him?" (Psalm 8:4). I suppose I feel the same way while surrounded by death. Like the power of creation, the totality of death makes me contemplate God.

What does the God of the living see when looking down on all these graves? God is the author of life and Creator of every single soul. Not one person is anonymous to God. If the soul never dies, then God never stops seeing anyone. What looks like hallowed ground to us is just another empty field to God.

As dark sky blanketed the cemetery, I returned to the warmth of my car, all the while struck by the obvious presence of God, no matter where on earth we go. We should all take time to go wherever it is we can see and hear God most clearly. For whatever reason, cemeteries are like that for me. There's no pretending in a cemetery, just reality as cold and hard as the stones that punctuate it. Death is frightening, but it is truth.

You might not think that going to a cemetery on Christmas makes a lot of sense, but it's perfect if you want to think about eternity. At Christmas, God came to earth to live the human life that we needed him to live. Jesus willingly went from a stable to a cross to a tomb. A cemetery. Except I believe he didn't stay put, and so that divine death is the key to reconnecting us with heaven and that peace we seek.

A writer I know named Andy got me thinking about God as a survivor in a zombie apocalypse. From God's perspective, this world of pain, suffering, and death is a complete disaster zone compared to what was originally intended. The analogy gets interesting when you consider how most survivors have to run and hide or turn and fight. Their actions are defined by desperation and fear. God is not just a survivor but the Creator, and he chose a different way to manage the apocalypse of humanity.

CHAPTER 7

THE SAVIOR

Death ends a life, not a relationship.

—Jack Lemmon

Thirty-three Chilean miners captivated the world in the fall of 2010, when they survived underground longer than anyone else in recorded history. Initially, the situation appeared grim. The men had been trapped after seven hundred thousand tons of rock collapsed and entombed them nearly a half mile below ground. Rescuers couldn't even determine if the men were still alive for the first seventeen days after the accident, but after two months, the last trapped miner successfully emerged in a specially designed rescue capsule nicknamed *Phoenix*.

A rescue worker named Manuel Gonzalez was the first man

down and last one up. No one knew what would happen as he stepped into the rescue capsule, yet he vowed to stay underground with the trapped men until each one made it safely to the surface more than two thousand feet above. He went into that dark place, helped lead each person out, and waited until the very end so that the last trapped man could safely escape what had almost become his grave.

The crowd went wild as Gonazalez emerged from the narrow passage and stepped from the capsule. Pictures taken by Associated Press photographers show the former professional soccer player smiling as he turns to the crowd and takes a bow. Chilean President Sebastian Pinera asked Gonzalez what he was thinking during the long, lonely trip back to the surface. The courageous safety expert reportedly replied: "I was thinking that I hope this never happens again."[1]

That's quite an understatement and a beautiful picture of sacrifice.

The literal resurrection of Jesus is also a beautiful picture of sacrifice as well as the most famous story of a dead person coming back to life in history. It's the peg upon which all of Christianity hangs because if Jesus wasn't God, and didn't rise from the dead, then the foundation of Christianity crumbles. The entire Old Testament points ahead to God appearing on earth as the Messiah. The New Testament and all of Christendom points back to Jesus as the fulfillment of that expectation. The Apostle Paul put it this

---

1. Variations of this quote appear in dozens of accounts from news outlets around the world.

way: "Face it—if there's no resurrection for Christ, everything we've told you is smoke and mirrors, and everything you've staked your life on is smoke and mirrors" (1 Corinthians 15:14 *THE MESSAGE*).

It is interesting that Paul mentions mirrors because vampires are famous for not having a reflection, and those fanged devils are exactly what I've been thinking about lately in relation to the execution of Jesus. Stick with me here.

VAMPIRES AND THE CROSS

It all starts with blood. Blood is a central theme throughout the Bible. All the way back in Genesis 4 God says that Abel's blood cries out from the ground after he is killed by his brother, Cain. Jewish teaching is filled with the idea that life flows through the blood. ("The life of every creature is its blood," Leviticus 17:14). It's involved in commandments, Passover, and the covenant God made with the Israelites. The Psalms talk repeatedly of bloodthirsty men. We're just scratching the surface here.

Blood is also central to vampire lore. The one thing vampires on the wrong side of death need more than anything else is blood. Christianity and vampire traditions share the concept that immortality comes through blood. Not a coincidence. Despite a wide variety of folklore across almost every culture in recent centuries, our Hollywood-reinforced myths tend to play up the ways in which vampires were often put at odds with the church. Some of these connections—vulnerability to holy water or crucifixes, for example—

were designed to depict such creatures as pure evil. But blood is still fundamental. The blood of Christ gives life whereas vampires take blood to have life or unlife or whatever you call being alive even though you're really dead. Jesus had to come back from the dead so that his innocent blood would allow others to live. Vampires come back from the dead to take lives, often innocent victims.

Strange traditions aren't just limited to bizarre stories centered on the Catholic church. Even Jesus raised eyebrows in Capernaum once by endorsing what sounded a lot like cannibalism. He baffled listeners by saying, "Whoever eats my flesh and drinks my blood has eternal life . . . for my flesh is real food and my blood is real drink" (John 6:54-55).

Those words weren't just shocking and confusing, they were offensive, a complete violation of Jewish law. The people took the commands of the Old Testament seriously including the one where God said, "None of you may eat blood."[2] Many of the men who had considered themselves followers of Jesus to this point could not accept crazy cannibalism ideas. They left. Speaking for Christians I can tell you how we often take strange-sounding statements for granted. We shouldn't expect everything we say to make sense to anyone who hears it. Some of the stuff Jesus said was *way* out there like this business about eating his flesh and drinking his blood, which was enough to send some of the disciples packing.[3] In fact, even his own brothers didn't believe his claims of divinity.

2. This rule is repeated multiple times in Leviticus 17:10-14 and is mentioned again in Deuteronomy 12:16.
3. Not the original Twelve. See John 6:60-69.

For the record, the restriction against drinking blood wasn't just divine whimsy. Those who followed the ancient code were spared ingesting any diseases that are carried through blood, practical advice millennia before modern medicine told us as much. Also, a lot of pagan cultures believed that eating the blood of an animal gave you its powers. For one, it doesn't, but God also wanted his people to rely on him as their source of strength.

Blood is precious, and throughout history we've understood the intimate connection that occurs when it is transferred from one person to another. According to biblical teaching, the blood of Christ is something to be accepted in a spiritual sense, an act of faith that's said to begin a relationship. Intimacy. Once again vampire legends often pervert the nature of intimacy through the transmittal of blood with sexual overtones and acts that feature lust in place of holiness.

I've always enjoyed the *Blade* movies, Marvel's franchise about a special vampire who capitalizes on his invincibility to sunlight by hunting regular vampires anytime he likes, daytime included. The storyline to *Blade Trinity*—the final film in the trilogy—takes the flip-flopping of Christian theology to an extreme. The story is about the original vampire, Dracula, who is dug up by some ambitious minions. Some of the younger ghouls even consider him to be a vampire messiah of sorts.

Blade works with a group of hunters who aim to rid the world of those evil, blood-sucking fiends (present company excluded of course when Blade's around). To that end they develop a virus capable of killing every vampire in the world. That is, if they can combine said virus with the blood of Dracula whose DNA is pure.

Unfortunately that guy is not cooperative, extremely terrifying, and supernaturally strong. You don't have to be a seminary student to pick up on some overlaps to Christian teachings here. But notice once again how the concept of messianic blood is present. Whereas the blood of Christ gives life to all humankind, the blood of Dracula in this story brings death to every creature created in his image. That's one way to look at it. But if you consider that the blood of Dracula kills all those nasty vampires then it really is something that is saving human lives. The tension is instant because there is no way you can get the blood you need without getting close.

UP CLOSE AND PERSONAL

Jesus of Nazareth said he was God, a blasphemous thing to do unless he was, in fact, telling the truth. He repeatedly told his followers that he must suffer and die to fulfill the mission of his ministry. He also declared that he would rise again, even though no one seemed to realize that he was talking about a literal death and resurrection.[4] He lived and died at the hands of Roman authorities. It's worth noting that these facts are verifiable outside of the New Testament accounts written by his followers.[5]

---

4. So when he figuratively says to eat his flesh and blood they take him literally. When he says he will literally rise from the dead they think he's being figurative. Fascinating.

5. The most famous historian on this topic is probably Josephus, an aristocratic Jew who earned Roman citizenship and chronicled life in the first century among other topics. His work *Antiquities of the Jews,* for example, has a couple of references to Jesus.

What a story. Just one day after having dinner with Lazarus, Martha, and Mary (who offered her gift of expensive perfume), Jesus rode into Jerusalem on a donkey. The crowds greeted him as a hero, but many of the people who mobbed him with praise would turn bloodthirsty in less than a week's time. He faced betrayal and rejection from within his core leadership group and finally suffered torture and death by one of the most terrible forms of execution ever devised. And he faced all of this alone. Most of his disciples fled. Those who remained had to watch from a distance. In the end, even God turned away. Jesus lingered there between heaven and hell, thirsting, as his lungs filled with fluid and his human heart slowly stopped beating.

A Roman soldier confirmed death by thrusting a spear through his side and into his chest cavity. Then Joseph of Arimathea, an influential disciple who owned a new tomb nearby, took the body. With the help of Nicodemus, a Pharisee who followed Jesus, Joseph prepared the body of his teacher with fresh linens and spices purchased for the burial. The resting place had been cut out of rock. Mary Magdalene watched as Joseph had a large stone rolled against the entrance of the tomb.

That appeared to be the end of the story. The supposed Savior was dead. Hopes and dreams were dashed. The disciples went into hiding amid a somber Jewish Sabbath. The darkness that fell over the land at the time of Jesus' death appeared to be a permanent fixture in the bleak skies over Palestine. For two days, nothing changed.

For those who left everything to follow Jesus, absolute despair descended after the crucifixion. They didn't see any reason to be hopeful. Resurrections didn't happen. The devastated followers of Jesus felt their dreams die with him. They were scared, unable to move, wondering what to do next. The one they believed in was dead, and they faced a real possibility of being found and punished as supporters of an insurrectionist. They doubted everything he taught them. They struggled with feelings of regret and failure over their inability to help the man who had done so much for them. Peter must have been extra sick after denying and cursing his Lord, just as Jesus had predicted he would.

We all struggle with feelings of despair, doubt, and guilt in our faith. That was no different for the disciples. But something changed between the days they hid in that secret room and the time when they would all face their own death for their faith. Besides Judas Iscariot—who betrayed Jesus and took his own life shortly after—all but one of the disciples was executed for preaching the resurrection of Jesus. Only John lived a full life without being martyred, and he still spent the end of his life as an exiled prisoner after facing some tough persecution of his own.[6] The disciples claimed to have seen their friend and leader alive and well after he had been murdered and buried. Their conviction changed the course of history. The only explanation that makes sense is that they were transformed, brought back to spiritual life.

6. Christian tradition holds that John miraculously survived being placed in a cauldron of boiling oil without being harmed.

UNDEAD MAYHEM AND THE RESURRECTION

We've spent a few chapters looking at fantastical biblical events that rival anything in pop culture. But perhaps nothing is as wild as a crazy event recorded by Matthew. He describes the earthquake that took place as Jesus died. What he says happened next deserves to be on a movie screen.

"At that moment the curtain of the temple was torn in two from top to bottom. The earth shook and the rocks split. The tombs broke open and the bodies of many holy people who had died were raised to life. They came out of the tombs, and after Jesus' resurrection they went into the holy city and appeared to many people" (Matthew 27:51-53).

Are you kidding me? I don't remember ever hearing this story when I was growing up.[7] How do you skip something so cool? And look at the timing of the whole thing. At the moment of Jesus' death, an earthquake broke open the tombs and blackness fell over the land. At some point during that darkness the dead people buried in sepulchres came to life, but the horde of undead saints didn't descend upon the town for two more days.

I'm picturing hands bursting from graves and decaying fingers slithering out from inside crypts like the iconic zombies waking up in "Thriller" while Michael Jackson dances and flashes those white socks for his girl. That's the type of scene Matthew paints in his Gospel. These sepulchres were carved from thick, heavy stone, not

---

7. OK, maybe I was distracted by eating glue, but I guarantee Miss Betty wasn't covering zombies of the Gospels on her flannelgraph board.

easily broken. Apparently God cracked them open like eggshells to use these dead people as further proof of his power.

Most Bible scholars don't even know what to say about this passage. We don't know who these dead people were who came back to life. We're not told who they appeared to in the city or where they went after these appearances. Did they visit loved ones or old enemies? Did they talk? Did they just walk down the road or vanish in some magnificent display? All we know is that one serious earthquake punctuated the magnitude of Christ's death. In the eighteenth-century, commentator Matthew Henry offered a few thoughts on the incident, but my favorite line of his is this: "The earth *quaked*, as if it *feared to open its mouth* to *receive* the blood of Christ."[8]

The moment also struck terror in the hearts of Jesus' executioners. Remember how tough these guys were? Unflinching soldiers of the ancient Roman guard. Even the centurion in charge of the entire operation uttered his famous response during the earthquake, an exclamation of faith that not even the disciples understood at the time: "Surely he was the Son of God."

I recently heard a story of a young Sunday school student who listened intently to the teacher describing how Jesus died and came back to life. Without any smirk or irony the young boy responded "you mean like a zombie?" Even honest seekers of truth get their lines crossed about Easter and the living dead due to the culturally iconic undead. Plenty of people have also mocked Jesus

8. Matthew Henry, *An Exposition of the Old and New Testament* vol. IV (New York: Robert Carter and Brothers, 1776).

by using the ever-popular zombie metaphor. More than twenty-five thousand people have liked Zombie Jesus on Facebook. You can even buy Zombie Jesus merchandise. Business always picks up around Easter each year. Special effects twist traditional pictures of Jesus for maximum effect. We mostly react by laughing or cringing. It's not so surprising, really. If you've never heard about the Bible, or how a man named Jesus died and came back to life, then zombies kind of make sense to be the first thing you'd think of in our undead-saturated culture. Jesus is the anti-zombie, really. He came back from the dead to give life, not to take it. But we all come to our own conclusions. Personally, I know of no other way to ultimately discuss spiritual life and death than through the divinity claims of Jesus. He brought life to his followers, and they were transformed.

It's hard not to make decisions based on emotion. This goes for skeptics and believers alike. We get so worked up into an emotional experience that we put our trust into whatever makes us feel good, God and Christianity included, even though we have no intellectual basis for our belief. Without the proper intellectual or emotional perspective, God is misunderstood and misrepresented.

One man I can really relate to is Thomas, one of the guys in Jesus' inner circle. Unfortunately, Thomas is often remembered negatively as the disciple who didn't believe that Jesus had come back to life (Thomas apparently had really bad timing and had stepped out for a moment when Jesus appeared to all his buddies). He said he wouldn't believe unless he saw the wounds in the hands and side of Jesus.

There's even a song, something about how we shouldn't be a doubting Thomas. I kind of wish I had never heard it. Thomas did not accept hearsay when others told him what they had experienced. It's simply not enough. We can't put our faith into how other people think or feel, either. Thomas wanted to examine the evidence for himself and have his own personal encounter with the risen Savior. Peter and the other disciples had the same response. When the women said Jesus was alive, the disciples thought the story was nonsense, yet we never beat them up for a lack of faith. When Jesus appeared in their room a second time, Thomas saw the evidence he so desperately wanted. He immediately believed that Jesus was God and spent the rest of his days serving as a missionary and gave his life as a martyr to the name of Christ.

We need to be more of a doubting Thomas so we find evidence to base our faith on and not just believe in something because it occasionally gives us warm fuzzies. Jesus warned us about the blind leading the blind. Chronic confusion and unchecked doubt are two pillars of spiritual death. We can't deny everything any more than we can blindly accept anything.

WELCOME TO LIFE

I'm what you call a hugger. There's really nothing like a great big bear hug, especially when you're feeling down. I bet after the shock of Jesus' appearance, there were some serious bear hugs in the upper room. Those hugs with Jesus carried immediate physical and emotional significance for the men and women who thought they would never see him again. Physically, that hug with Jesus provided tangible evidence that he really had risen from the dead. Emotionally, the touch conveyed his love for each individual who embraced him.

News cameras recorded many hugs in Chile in 2010 as those miners emerged one by one from what many feared would be their grave. Of all the joys we can experience, nothing matches the feeling of trading death for life. As one of the miners emerged from the darkness, he was greeted by President Pinera who said, "Welcome to life."

God remains a mystery to us on many levels. The one thing we really get is this: It was all about connecting with us. That's what the resurrection—this story of a dead guy returning to life—is all about. We are naturally disconnected from him, so he came up with a way to bridge the gap. Maybe we're so fascinated with undead beings, like zombies and vampires, because we inherently understand that the solution to our problems comes from someone coming back to life in perfection and actually defeating death.

The Chilean miners experienced an awakening much like a spiritual awakening. We were trapped in a dark tomb, but God paid a high price to get in the tomb and rescue us. We don't have to wait until we are cleaned up or even able to clearly see what exactly happened. We just have to reach up and embrace the cross as it was offered to us. And when we emerge from that black pit and into the light, it's like God gives us a great big bear hug and says, "Welcome to life."

CHAPTER 8

THE FACE OF DEATH

So some of him lived but the most of him died—(Even as you or I!)
—Rudyard Kipling

The first time I witnessed a person's last breath was with my grandma, who had cancer. We knew it was coming for weeks. On a Friday night in November I took a date to a movie. About twenty minutes into the film, my phone buzzed. I left my date and went straight over to the nursing home. It wasn't going to be much longer.

My sister and I sat alongside my grandmother's bed through the night and whispered around as she was delirious with death. The smell that accompanies such a scene never leaves your memory. I wish I could have done something more than watch her fall asleep forever. I held her hand and felt the transition take place, the exact moment when she ceased to be a living person.

It was very similar, a little over a year later, when my grandfather died in that same place. A bit bolder, I took his hand fully in mine and willed him to squeeze as hard as he could if only to take a fraction of the fear away from whatever it was that was happening in his heart, mind, and soul.

When someone dies, we never forget the look on their face, color draining from their skin, mouth agape as it struggles to find one more breath. But the eyes stand out most of all. They seem to go somewhere distant. We call them the windows to our soul, so maybe that look at the time of death is like a window opening to let eternity in.

BURIED ALIVE

A long time ago there was a cruel form of execution called immurement—the more common term is being walled. People condemned to immurement were stuck behind a wall that would be built over them. Victims would die of starvation or dehydration. It had to be as terrible as it sounds. It's killing someone without having to actually kill them. Creepy.

An old television movie called *Buried Alive* told the tale of a bad wife and her doctor boyfriend, who came up with a plan to kill her husband. Their exotic murder weapon of choice was a fatal neurotoxin that can be extracted from a puffer fish. Poor Tim

Matheson never saw it coming. He unwittingly drank the poison, died, and was buried. Alive.[1]

The poison, called tetrodotoxin, has actually been the secret ingredient of many Voodoo priests in Haiti, sort of the cradle of zombie civilization.[2] Just the right amount will make someone appear to be dead even though they're actually paralyzed, with almost undetectable vital signs. So why would a Voodoo priest want to poison someone to make it look like they're dead? To create mindless human pets. The community would believe said person was dead, and the sinister witchdoctor would hope to have control over a brain-damaged human. Almost all the people exposed to tetrodotoxin die, but if the bad guys try this enough they might eventually get a "real" zombie.

What does all this have to do with Tim Matheson? Well, he drank just enough to seem dead but not enough to really be dead, so of course he woke up inside a coffin in a macabre and very memorable scene. The not-so-murdered husband finds his way home to take his revenge.

Now, what does Tim Matheson have to do with spiritual death?

Being immured, or buried alive, is pretty high up on the list of most terrifying ways to die. But we often suffer spiritual death in a similar way. Some people might turn abruptly, but most of us just slip away. It's gradual. We don't intend to make certain decisions

---

1. Insert dramatic pause and maniacal laugh here.

2. We get the word *zombie* from the Haitians who got it from West Africa. For a good overview of all things zombie check out Nathan Robert Brown, *The Complete Idiot's Guide to Zombies* (New York: Alpha, 2010).

that leave us empty and feeling alone; we just end up at that point. We look back, trying to figure out where God was and what path we were even on. It's kind of like spiritual starvation or dehydration, which makes sense when we consider that Jesus called himself the bread of life and living water.

In *Surprised by Joy*, C. S. Lewis describes the process—both conscious and unconscious—of abandoning God to become an atheist during his adolescence. He described what happened after he started attending a new boarding school. "I ceased to be a Christian. The chronology of this disaster is a little vague, but I know for certain that it had not begun when I went there and that the process was complete very shortly after I left."[3]

Spiritual immurement might not be the most violent process, but it's deadly just the same. We find ourselves behind walls that keep us from God, whether we build them ourselves or allow others to do it for us. We're chained to things that keep us from the sustenance of life that God offers. In that spiritual sense, we slowly die behind obstructions of self-love or addiction or whatever it is that buries us alive.

It's often hard to recognize the face of death in our own lives. We don't see it so clearly when we are the ones on spiritual life support. Undead monsters make a great metaphor for spiritual death because decaying zombies and eternally damned vampires symbolize the opposite of purity and holiness, which is the essence of God. It's a lot easier to go into denial rather than face the frightening reality.

---

3. C. S. Lewis, *Surprised by Joy* (London: Fontana Books, 1967), 52.

DEATH AND PANCAKES

A brilliant movie called *Stranger than Fiction* tells the story of a man named Harold Crick, who leads a mundane existence. Until one day, he hears the narrator of his life calmly declare his imminent death.

He freaks out. But then he seeks out an English literature professor for advice. The professor says too bad; Harold doesn't control his own fate and can't do anything about it, so he might as well go have an adventure or just eat pancakes every day. Harold wants to know who in the world would choose eating pancakes over living. The professor says that it all depends on how good both the life and pancakes are.

Think of God as the narrator of our lives. We struggle with the balance between our will and his control. But even though we know that we're going to die, we're not just left to whatever we feel like doing, even if that means eating nothing but pancakes. Our goal is to live the life that we were created to live. God has a plan, and we each fulfill a specific purpose. We can try living our lives our way, but it won't even be as good as if we just ate pancakes all the time. Even if they had whipped cream on them.

Here's the thing: We can't really live to the fullest until we're ready to die. The deaths of my grandparents only a year apart led me to think a great deal about life and death. I made some really big—and ultimately bad—decisions during that time. I guess I just wanted something exciting and new to erase the specter of death. But focusing on the fragility of life isn't the same as coming to grips with it. Understanding the reality of death is only a start.

THE MEANING OF DEATH

It's good to think about death if we optimistically focus on eternity; bad if we become fatalists.

My friend Kim had a professor who made his students write their own obituaries. Then he had them plan their own funeral including songs, pallbearers, and more. Steven Covey does a similar exercise in *The 7 Habits of Highly Effective People*. There's a reason that effective people consider their funerals. Ironically, understanding and accepting physical death is a key to attaining spiritual life.

Maybe it's good to sort of rehearse dying. Normally, the only way to conquer a fear is to confront and overcome it. As children we learn that certain things in life aren't so bad once we attempt them. We never think about training wheels again once we learn how to speed all over the neighborhood on a bike. Same goes for roller coasters, driving, and parenting. Our fear of these things fades once we meet them head on. But we don't get to do that with death. Wouldn't it be nice if we could practice dying, just try it out to see how we do, like Bill Murray's character in *Groundhog Day*?

It's amusing when people say, "I thought I was going to die," as if they're not still going to. We don't even like to think about death, but according to the ancient King Solomon, we should. "For you are going to die, and you should think about it while there is still time" (Ecclesiastes 7:2 NLT). The wise old king must have been quite a realist. What gives?

Death is the ultimate enemy, certainly not attractive but undoubtedly compelling. A lot of us watch *Final Destination* movies even though we know how they're going to end. Some psychologists argue that our entire lives are subconsciously controlled by our preoccupation with death. This fear is often married to anxiety over suffering, pain, and loss. Most of us fear death because it's the end. After that comes the great unknown, and we all wonder what it's really like. If the promises of God are true, we can actually be excited about what comes after this life, especially the heaven part. But our human understanding is limited to a finite perspective that makes the concept of eternity scary.

Solomon made it clear that we all have to face forever. God made it clear from the beginning of time when he "planted eternity in the human heart" (Ecclesiastes 3:11 NLT). The conflict over our impending demise is that we know we must die yet have eternity in our hearts. We consider death to be a natural part of life, but something in us knows that wasn't God's plan for creation. Life preceded death, and no one can escape that fact through science, theology, or any other means.

In the New Testament, Paul also struggled with issues of death and the corruption of human nature when he asked, "Who will rescue me from this body of death?" (Romans 7:24). James says that desire conceives and gives birth to sin, which leads to death. In this existence, mortality is part of the package. The situation is grim, downright fatal, even, when we look squarely into the reality of it.

Our desire to live is as natural as the inevitability of death. My favorite rendition of Charles Dickens's iconic character Ebenezer Scrooge is played by Bill Murray in *Scrooged*, who is taken to his future funeral by the Ghost of Christmas Future. When he finds himself locked inside a coffin slowly sliding into the flames he cries and screams over and over "I want to live!"

Some of us believe we can cheat and possibly beat death, maybe even years after dying. More than one hundred people have even paid the Alcor Life Extension Foundation thousands of dollars to freeze their bodies, in some cases just their heads,[4] in hopes that scientists will one day develop ways to cure nasty diseases such as cancer. This process is called cryogenics in which "patients" are frozen.[5] Alcor took another seven, um, patients in during 2011. In case some of you nitpicky people are wondering what good it would do to come back as nothing more than a head you must realize that science may one day be able to use molecular technology to grow entire new bodies.

Certainty of death simply isn't going to stop humankind from trying. In some cases we're even finding success. Researchers at the University of Pittsburgh were thrilled in 2005 after finding a way to revive dogs three hours after clinical death.[6] The international tabloid media picked up the story and applied the sensational title of "zombie dogs" even if the scientists involved didn't appreciate the metaphor.

The goal of this remarkable project was to put living creatures into a state of suspended animation (barely alive) so that emergency responders would have more time to save the lives of trauma

---

4. I keep picturing Richard Nixon in *Futurama*.
5. I prefer to call these "patients" dead people or corpses.
6. One place this is referenced is the *New York Times*, www.nytimes.com/2005/12/11/magazine/11ideas_section4-21.html

victims dying from severe blood loss. Sounds completely sci-fi, but the process involves injecting a cold solution into the victim's circulatory system in order to dramatically lower the body temperature and keep the patient in a temporarily frozen, kind-of-alive-but-not-quite state (think Han Solo in carbonite). And it worked! At least on some of the dogs. Workers at Massachusetts General Hospital also succeeded with similar testing on pigs and mice.

Something about zombie mice freaks me out more than dogs, and zombie bacon probably wouldn't even taste good, but these researchers are doing amazing work to help people. They are trying to re-create the miraculous cases that occasionally take place in nature by inducing hibernation in dying humans. Ironically, stopping someone's life in the correct way will give doctors time to provide the necessary treatment so that the patient can be reanimated in a controlled way.

So we hold this longing for life yet struggle with mortality. But Paul also points to the solution: "So now there is no condemnation for those who belong to Christ Jesus. For the power of the life-giving Spirit has freed you through Christ Jesus from the power of sin that leads to death" (Romans 8:1-2 NLT).

Those of us who put our faith in the work of the cross can look forward to the inevitability of life rather than the inevitability of death.

A band named Evanescence broke out a few years ago after releasing a song called "Bring Me to Life." It always makes me think of my faith, especially after I realized what the lyrics actually said. It's about being asleep in the dark and how there has to be something more to life than numb deadness. Vocalist Amy Lee sings about this person who's always been right there in front of her even though she could never see who it was. There can be life among the dead, but it takes the touch of this savior, someone who will call her by name to wake her, save her, bring her back to life.

When our days get black enough, we can even turn on God because we just don't care anymore. At least we think we don't care. When I hear that song, I think of myself in the darkness, and picture Christ as the one before me. His call and touch bring us back to life.

SEEING DEAD PEOPLE

An old friend of mine named Dave died recently. Cancer. He was my age, a great guy with a heart you could feel and a smile that made you believe.

Dave and I weren't always close, just always connected. Every time we saw each other we would hug and smile and catch up on where we were heading in life. We were teenagers together in the same church and twenty-something college students together at the same university. We were also guys at some of the same parties, both of us uncomfortable in the shared knowledge of a God who knew we weren't giving our best in those days.

Then some years passed, a few random encounters in between, and we were once again reconnected. We had both changed after going through our own personal apocalypses. His was much more severe, a tragic diagnosis that would ultimately prove inescapable. One beautiful summer morning we met up, and he was smiling. I wondered how sick he really was and if I might hurt him when we hugged. I asked him how he was doing. He told me God was good. *Good.* What is that anyway? We always talk about the good life. It used to mean something about money or status or at least a lot of people who thought we were cool. But a good God is not the same thing as a good life, to most people. And when someone who is dying tells you that God is good, you don't forget it.

Sometimes life feels like a cosmic vending machine. There's a lot of nice stuff in there like great friends and love, but there are also nasty selections like cancer and divorce. Sometimes we directly push buttons for some of the bad stuff, but other times we push the button for happiness and instead end up with our hopes and dreams stuck on the ledge like a teetering Snickers bar while something horrible, like a car wreck, falls to us.

Dave and I ran into each other again only a couple months before he died. He was leaving a youth football game that he had just refereed. He looked thin, but told me he felt OK. He told me God is in control. At those words, my faith strengthened and my heart broke at the same time.

A lot of people ask questions about the meaning of life or why I'm a "Jesus weirdo" or how a good God could allow so much suffering to happen. Answers to these kinds of tough questions often flip to autopilot, like some processor that computes objections and responds with appropriate points of logic and evidence. But lost in that is the emotion, the rawness of the experience of doubt. Part of being a spiritual zombie is hitting that autopilot mode, which is bad, because we forget what a struggle this business of faith in God really is. The best we can do most of the time is try to imagine what God's perspective must be like.

During one climactic scene of *The Walking Dead*, a character named Andrea decides to end her life. She can't handle the terror of existing among the undead anymore. The group is evacuating a government facility that will soon self-destruct, but Andrea decides to stay with a couple of others who have chosen a brief, painless death by incineration rather than fighting to survive the zombie apocalypse any longer. An older character named Dale cares about her and refuses to let her stay and die. He doesn't fight her or get physical in any way but rather sits down next to her and says if she dies then he does too. He refuses to leave her side, so she escapes with him and lives.

And she hates him for it.

She won't talk to him and treats him like dirt after that. When he finally confronts her, she lashes out in anger. She wanted to die. That was her choice, and he had no right to stop her. Stunned and hurt, Dale can only say, "I saved your life."[7]

If we get angry over terrible things happening on earth we can ball our fists toward heaven and yell, "How could you?!" What does that look like to the Creator of those balled fists? Maybe God just looks back at us and says, "But I saved you."

---

7. These scenes are also from the "TS-19" episode that I referenced in chapter 1.

The most heartbreaking part of the cross for Jesus was the full knowledge of every person who would ever choose death in place of his love.

A friend and I went together to the funeral home for Dave's viewing. Mourners waited in line for hours to pay tribute to his life and family. We could see his body in the casket for the last fifteen minutes of waiting in line. There's nothing right about looking at a thirty-three-year-old man in a casket. It was very sad.

As we reached the front of the line, Dave's parents were there to greet us. I hugged his mom, who was more comforting to me than I could be to her. My friend was visibly downcast as he spoke with Dave's dad, staring at his clasped hands, not sure what to say. But Dave's father put his arm around my friend's shoulder and said, "No, look at that." He directed our attention past the casket and pointed to a beautiful painted portrait in the corner of the room. It almost looked like a photograph, this image of Dave smiling back at us. "Doesn't he look good?"

It was a beautiful moment. We were sad and thinking about the death, but Dave's dad saw him as being alive and better than ever. We remember how people were in the good times so that we can block out the painful memories of weakness and death.

That scene is a picture of the way it is with us and God. Jesus became the ultimate slate wiper for us. God puts his arm around us, points to a picture of Christ, and says, "No, no, no. *That's* what I see when I look at you. I don't see your sadness and failure and death. I see my Son. Alive."

That's why Jesus means so much to me, and I believe that's why my dying friend could say that God is good. We don't have to fear the face of death once we clearly see the face of God.

CHAPTER 9

THE SERVANT

God pours life into death and death into life without a drop being spilled.

—Anonymous

Legendary magician Harry Houdini spent much of his career exposing frauds and charlatans who claimed to have the supernatural ability to speak to the dead. Through natural means, Houdini could duplicate every trick his challengers used to allegedly communicate with spirits beyond the grave.

In 1926, Houdini survived being buried alive for an hour and a half. He performed the stunt to debunk an Egyptian man named Rahman Bey who claimed to do a similar feat through supernatural abilities. The dangerous stunt required the escape artist to be placed in a sealed casket, which was then submerged in the swimming pool of the Hotel Shelton in New York. The fifty-two-year-old performed the feat a second time in Massachusetts that year, just one month before his sudden death on Halloween. A bronze casket had been prepared so that Houdini could perform a stage version of the effect in 1927. Ironically, that casket was used to transport Houdini's body home from Detroit, where he had died from appendicitis.

I wonder what Houdini would have thought of Peter, the leader of Jesus' disciples. Peter burst onto the scene in a miraculous way with flaming tongues that would make a Pink Floyd show look like a two-year-old's Lite-Brite display.[1]

Following the resurrection and ascension of Jesus, thousands of people became followers of the living Christ as they watched Peter and company preach and act in the supernatural power of the Holy Spirit. Unexplainable phenomena occurred throughout Judea. Even a man named Simon the Sorcerer—the Houdini of his day—believed in the power of God and was baptized. Finally, Peter performed the most amazing of all the acts performed by any disciple.

A ROCKY BEGINNING

Handpicked by Jesus right off the shore of Galilee, Peter was the undisputed leader of the pack, a dynamo in Jesus' inner circle

---

1. I'm referring to the wild happenings at Pentecost recorded in Acts 2.

who succeeded and failed in big ways. He was loud, and at times obnoxious, speaking boldly for what he believed and eventually giving his life for those beliefs.

Peter experienced the most incredible moments of Jesus' ministry. He was in the room when Jairus's daughter was raised from the dead, and he witnessed one of the most ghostly events in the New Testament: the transfiguration of Jesus.

After Jesus began explaining that he would eventually be put to death, he took Peter, James, and John up to a mountaintop. While Peter and his friends looked on, Jesus began to shine brighter than anything they had ever seen. His face became like the sun, his clothes its reflection. Suddenly, Moses and Elijah—both of them dead for centuries—showed up and began talking with Jesus. Luke says that they spoke about the upcoming trials Jesus would face in Jerusalem. As the Old Testament legends left, a cloud descended upon the disciples, who were scared out of their minds. Then the voice of God spoke. "This is my Son, whom I love. Listen to him!" (Mark 9:7).

This wasn't like seeing the face of Jesus in a grilled cheese sandwich or a Dorito or all the other bizarre places people claim to see God.[2] The word *transfiguration* describes a metamorphosis into something more glorious. Peter, James, and John were permitted to witness Jesus in a form so perfect and beautiful that the earth could hardly contain such a presence.

Jesus gave the men strict instructions to keep what they had seen to themselves until he had risen from the dead. They obeyed

---

2. Of course, if the Almighty really wants to hang out in someone's lunch or on paneled walls, then I guess he can.

and maintained their silence even though they still had no clue what "rising from the dead" even meant. So they panicked when Jesus was arrested in the Garden of Gethsemane, put on trial, and killed the next morning. Confused and frightened, Peter denied ever knowing the condemned Jesus and even called down curses upon his friend before going into hiding. Shocking behavior from the man Jesus called the Rock upon which he would build his earthly kingdom. In that moment, the Rock crumbled under pressure.

Peter must have hated himself by Easter morning, when the women showed up shouting about how Jesus was missing. It must have been hard to face the one he personally rejected, but he embraced his Lord and a chance at redemption. Jesus honored their commitment and let Peter lead the way in the postresurrection world.

On the day of Pentecost, a major Jewish festival, the disciples were all together when bizarre things started happening. Luke describes a wild, haunted house–like scene. The spirit of God blew through with the sound of a hurricane. Tongues of fire appeared and fell upon them, and language barriers disappeared. The spectacle attracted visitors from many different cultures who were able to understand what the disciples were saying. And guess who stepped up to speak to thousands of assembled celebrants. Peter, the man who less than two months earlier had denied even knowing Jesus.

Miracles continued. Through the power of God's spirit, Peter healed the sick and disabled, just as Jesus had done. Those miserable days of fear and betrayal faded. Peter rocked so many miracles that people raced into the streets just to see him. Some people placed sick friends along the public throughways in hopes that even his shadow might fall on them. While some thought these healings were magic or sorcery, those who listened to Peter knew that he credited all the amazing feats to a higher power. God works through many people, from the high profile disciples to unassuming servants like an unheralded first-century saint named Tabitha, whose story is told in the book of Acts (9:32-43).

THE GAZELLE AND SPIRITUAL VAMPIRES

Tabitha lived in the Mediterranean seaport town of Joppa where she spent her life serving those around her like a first-century Mother Teresa.

In Greek, her name was Dorcas, which means gazelle, a deer-like creature. A godly woman, Tabitha was always doing good and helping the poor, living up to her name as a woman who kept moving. She was a saint, literally and figuratively, who was known for alsmdeeds, an old word that means acts of mercy and giving from whatever you have to help others.

Traditional acts of mercy included providing someone with food, clothing, a place to stay, or something to drink. We take for granted how many people could be thirsty in first-century Palestine. Many water sources were unfit for drinking, and the climate didn't help. Food and clothing were also in short supply for the neediest members of society. We don't know exactly what kind of resources Tabitha had, but she used them to help others. Her life showed that true faith isn't passive but active. After all, faith without works is dead (James 2:13-17).

In modern times, she would be at the retirement home checking in on adopted loved ones and playing cards with lonely seniors. She'd be dropping off a hot meal at the home of a family who had just lost a loved one. Being like Tabitha isn't easy. Getting involved in the lives of needy people is a full-time job that requires a lot of personal sacrifice. It means going out of our way to help people we could easily ignore. Society seems to say "It's not your problem. Just forget about him or her. Everyone else already has." Yet that's precisely the reason the Tabithas of the world take the time to care for others.

People who are totally selfless challenge us. Modern American society often encourages us to focus on ourselves. We can be selfish. Especially near the end of college, when our small problems, like where to work or where to live, take precedence over the struggles of others. Not to say that as early-twenty-somethings we don't give of ourselves, but the giving tends to come out of the fringes, whatever's leftover.

Selfishness is spiritual vampirism: living based on our needs rather than the needs of others. At its worst we can suck people dry and move on to the next victim, always looking for ways to get what we want no matter how many people get hurt in the process.[3] Countless vampire novels, films, and stories warn us: If you spend time with vampires, you'll either turn into one or they'll bleed you dry.

3. For a unique look at this idea check out a fun allegorical novel called *Night of the Living Dead Christian* (Carol Stream, Ill.: Tyndale, 2011) by the brilliant Matt Mikalatos.

We're more likely to sap someone else's energy when we're worn down. The grind of life tires us out sometimes. That's when it's easy to use up someone else's energy. Opportunities to help others who need us usually don't pop up when we're wide awake and have nowhere to go. We tend to bump into desperate people when we're in a hurry to get somewhere or as we crawl into bed at the end of a draining day and the phone starts ringing.

But there's one thing about giving and taking from others: Helping a person in need reinvigorates us. Our focus shifts during those times when we get it right and come through for a friend. We stop worrying about our problems and even get a second, third, or fourth wind. It makes no sense; our natural bodies should be exhausted. But giving is a spiritual thing. God holds an infinite supply of energy and injects us with some when we need it. These mysterious bursts of energy are better than a pot of coffee. It all comes back to the balance of wrongness and rightness we feel in our lives, that quest for inner peace that we refer to as spiritual life. Giving selflessly is right, and spiritual completeness somehow comes from doing so.[4]

Tabitha met needs deeper than just physical needs when she provided solace, counsel, and prayer. Often we just need a place to go, shelter from the storm, so to speak. Tabitha ministered to widows who faced loads of emotional struggles and needed strength. Life was tough enough for them, such as the woman at

---

4. I should mention that taking isn't always bad. We often need help from others and should accept gracious offers. Selfishly taking is a different story.

Nain who watched Jesus bring her son back to life. The situation was even worse for Christian widows by this time. Roman authorities escalated oppressive measures in the years following the resurrection of Jesus. Tabitha kept the widows going.

So after she became sick and died, her friends were utterly distraught. They washed her body and placed it in an upper room. Then they heard that Peter was only one town away, and the slightest hope flickered in that dark room.

PAGING PETER

Peter was preaching and healing people in a place called Lydda. Many people were turning to God, especially after seeing a man named Aeneas, who had been paralyzed for eight years, stand and walk. Peter's stay in Lydda was interrupted when Tabitha's frantic friends showed up. He wasn't being summoned to a funeral. He was being summoned so there *wouldn't be* a funeral.

This effort to get Peter shows great faith on the part of the Joppa believers. We don't know how much information the messengers gave to the apostle. Some commentators have suggested that they might have been vague, not even explaining that Tabitha was already dead. Peter's faith was strong, but traveling to another town to see a corpse was a much different thing than going to see a sick person.

In the Old Testament, the prophet Jonah fled to Tabitha's hometown of Joppa in defiance of God's command to go and preach to the people of Nineveh. Jonah went to Joppa out of disobedience; Peter went there in obedience. It's interesting how a particular location can be exactly where God wants one person yet the last place he expects another to be. Each one of us has a unique calling, but we can get into trouble when we start "discerning" the will of God just by watching where someone else goes or what someone else does. One person might be called to a foreign country whereas another might be called to the kitchen table. One person might be great at defending their faith in a pub whereas another could go to that same place and end up in rehab. Being wise always starts with looking to God for the next step. God called Peter to Joppa. And he went.

When Peter arrived on the scene, the mourners pleaded with him to do something. The widows surrounded him and showed off all the clothing Tabitha had made for them. They displayed the garments as if to say "Look at what she's done! We *need* her." The proof of her service was clearly visible. To them, losing Tabitha felt like losing a mother or sister.

For Peter's part, he might not have even known that the good woman was dead until this moment. He stood in an upper room, rattled by all the commotion, seeing the corpse left out for him, wondering what these people expected him to do. As he listened to the stories of the good woman's kindness and observed the work of her hands, a picture of a resourceful and greatly loved woman became clear. Like the fabrics Tabitha wove, her life became a beautiful tapestry.

If you speed read through this story, it's easy to miss the

weight of what's happening. This passage is short, and it reads as if Peter marched from Lydda right over to Joppa and raised this lady from the dead. But he didn't know what God would do.

Peter sent everyone out of the room, just as Jesus had done at the home of Jairus. The image of that little girl rising from death must have played over in his mind. But would something like that happen again? Alone in the room with a corpse, he prayed a prayer that likely contained some uncertainty. Knowing God can do anything doesn't mean that it *will* be done. Even as Peter was praying that God do something miraculous, it's highly possible that he wondered, *What if this doesn't work?* How would he explain to everyone that Tabitha was dead and there was nothing he could do about it?

The posture and positioning of Peter reinforces the challenges of faith that even he was subject to. First, he knelt. It's one instance in which he did not model the example of Jesus, who, according to what we can see in biblical accounts, never knelt before such a major miracle. The second thing to note is how he sits. Matthew Henry offered this insight: "*He turned to the body,* which intimates that when he prayed he turned from it; lest the sight of it should discourage his faith, he looked another way, to teach us . . . *against hope, to believe in hope,* and overlook the difficulties that lie in the way, *not considering the body as now dead,* lest we should *stagger at the promise.*"[5]

Peter turned away while praying so the sight of a corpse would not cause him to betray his faith. Jesus never had to doubt, but

---

5. Matthew Henry, *Commentary on the Whole Bible,* vol VI, *Acts to Revelation* (n.p., 1706).

Peter knew he wasn't in control. That's the problem with focusing on problems. If we stare at them all day, every day, it won't be long before we become paralyzed by fear and doubt. We need to focus on Peter's example, to focus on potential solutions instead.

Finally, Peter turned to the dead woman and said, "Tabitha, get up." She came to, saw Peter, and sat up. Sounds so normal. The image of her open eyes and brief disorientation makes the association with a gazelle even more fitting. Maybe the deer-in-the-headlights look aptly describes the momentary appearance of someone who was somewhere in the netherworld before suddenly finding herself back on planet earth. Coming back to life must be weird enough, let alone to do so and be staring at some bearded guy you've never seen before. But I have a feeling that Peter might have been freaking out more than her. Thinking, *I can't believe it actually worked.*

He took Tabitha by the hand and helped her to her feet. What a surreal moment. The only thing better than watching his new friend return from death was calling all of her old friends in to share in the euphoria. The widows and other believers rushed into the room to see if it was true, and the celebration was on.

STANDING IN THE GAP

My pastor friend Mike—who compared me to a quarterback—recently challenged us at church by asking whether or not anybody would miss us if we suddenly vanished from the community. Mike said there should be a hole in our cities and towns if we suddenly disappeared. I don't think he meant that churches should blow stuff up on their way out of town, just that we should be responding to needs that are often ignored. If we serve in the way that we're called to, we will affect lives around us.

The story of Tabitha demonstrates how God entrusts us to be his hands and feet and how we can have an impact on our communities and the world around us. The challenge is to be a selfless servant rather than a selfish vampire. It sounds a lot easier than it really is.

Helping others isn't only in grand gestures, big projects, and frantic needs. People everywhere are desperate and hurting. They long for companionship—a smile, a listening ear, an afternoon of comfort. Neighborhoods are filled with lonely souls, many of them elderly, who have no one to share their days with or even check in on them. Folks are so grateful when someone takes time to care about them. If we're more like Tabitha, then we'll leave plenty of holes when we disappear.

One of the best ways to be spiritually revitalized is to show kindness to others, especially those incapable of reciprocating, in the name of God. We're challenged every single time we think about what it takes to love other people as we love ourselves. Giving people are always willing to be intruded upon, as if they wore shirts that say "Interrupt me." Even though we don't mean to, we can often look like "Don't bother me" people.

Jesus welcomed everybody who looked to him for help. He was approachable and he demonstrated a heart for needy interrupters. One day, while walking from Jericho to Jerusalem, two blind men heard his entourage approaching and cried out for him to show them mercy. Some men in the crowd told the beggars to shut up, as if such lowly men should never bother the great teacher. But there's a great little phrase tucked away in Matthew 21:32 that says, "Jesus stopped and called them" (NIV). There isn't a person on the planet that Jesus wouldn't stop for out of compassion. He touched the eyes of the blind men and restored their sight.

God loves providing for us and easing our suffering, but he also wants us to do some work. We don't have to save the world in one fell swoop. God just wants us to do what we can wherever we are. I love that movie *Signs* about a family in Pennsylvania during an alien invasion. Quirks and skills of each character—a little girl who leaves glasses of water everywhere and a former baseball player, for example—are revealed along the way. At the end of the film we realize that they all play a significant role for their salvation. We are set up to have that same kind of impact. We just have to be willing to offer what we have to those around us who need it.

Like Harry Houdini exposing frauds during the search for something real all those years ago, people around the world seek someone who is genuine. We're so sick of fake everything. Sacrifices from the Tabithas of the world are like postcards from God, little reminders that it's not about us. Selfless acts of kindness provide a tiny glimpse of heaven.

Some of the happiest people I know have very few things. They know that time, their very lives, can either be invested or wasted, and they choose to invest in others. They spend less, give more, and find contentment at the heart of healthy spiritual living.

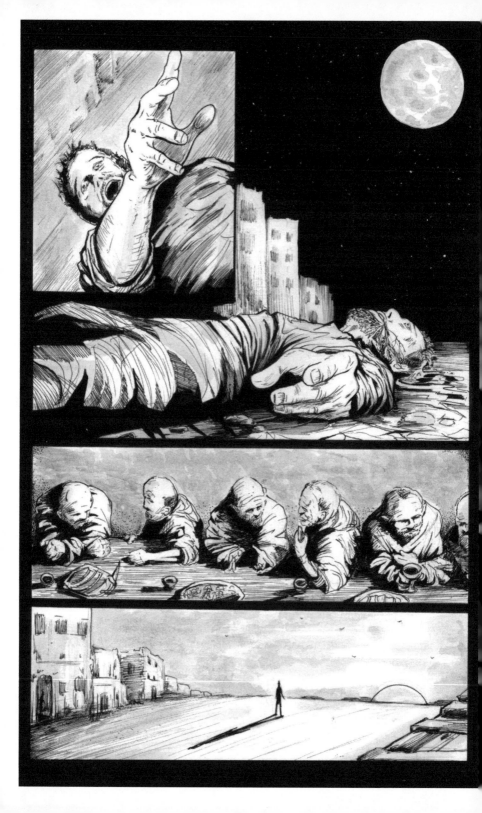

CHAPTER 10

THE STUDENT

Every parting gives a foretaste of death, every reunion a hint of the resurrection.

—Arthur Schopenhauer

Researchers recently discovered "zombie ants" in Thailand and the rainforest of Brazil. Amazing footage shows the bizarre behavior of afflicted insects as fungal spores infect their brains, take over their minds and bodies, and drive them away from the rest of the colony until the doomed creatures chomp down on the vein of a leaf that provides nourishment for the fungus. The insect dies, but the fungus flourishes and grows for a couple of weeks until bursting to release its deadly spores all over the area. If a fellow ant-colony member finds an infected ant with a compromised brain, the threat is immediately removed from the rest of the group. Entire colonies can be wiped out by this mind-controlling agent. The community must be protected.[1]

Creepy. In the recent renditions of certain undead creatures such as vampires, the romanticized versions of what were classically recognized as monsters often make us forget that the catalyst for their transformation is diseaselike, a virus for example. Once infected, vampires must leave their past life behind and abandon relationships they once held. Anne Rice's *Interview with the Vampire* highlights the transformation from life to undeath more than most other novels. Louis and the young Claudia are turned by Lestat. While Louis suffers the more violent transition of being attacked and bitten first, Claudia is turned with just a few drops of Lestat's vampire-tainted blood. As a result, they become wanderers forever detached from any kind of normal society. Mind control is a powerful thing, strong enough to turn humans into mere pets.

HOLLOWED OUT

The Apostle Paul warned us to guard our minds against intellectual attacks and outright lies. "See to it that no one takes you captive through hollow and deceptive philosophy, which depends on human tradition and the basic principles of this world rather than on Christ" (Colossians 2:8).

---

1. One particularly good article on this fascinating phenomenon is Wynne Parry's "How Zombie Ants Lose Their Minds" and can be found at www.livescience.com/14064-zombie-ant-fungus-parasite.html.

Paul's life was split into two main parts. In the first half of his life he was known as Saul, a violent persecutor of early Christians. After a Godly intervention, Saul became Paul, one of the best missionaries in history. God gave him the new name, which means "small" and indicates humility, one of the most important traits of a great leader. Paul would have made a great coach. In fact, that's kind of what he was. The people on his "team" relied on his game plan. When they screwed up, he dropped the hammer on them. When they lost heart, he encouraged them.

As an itinerant preacher, Paul traveled widely throughout the ancient Mediterranean world and planted many churches. He had been globetrotting for years and was in the middle of his third major missionary journey, the busiest one yet. This particular swing took him as far north as Macedonia—birthplace of Alexander the Great—and as far south as Jerusalem, where Jesus had gone to die. Paul did some of the greatest writing in history during this trek, including his two most well-known letters to the Corinthians as well as what became the books of Galatians and Romans.

Things turned sour in Ephesus when a group of townspeople formed a mob and targeted Paul's friends. Apparently, the appealing message of Jesus' love was bad for the business of silversmiths, who sold icons for worshiping pagan gods. Luke, the author of Acts, describes multiple instances when enemies of God hatched plots to take Paul out. That's what happened after the trouble in Ephesus, so Paul and his friends decided to backtrack through Macedonia rather than sail south to Syria.

They ended up in Troas, a key port city at the crossroads of Asia Minor and Europe. The place had so much glitz and glamour that the great emperor Constantine would later consider making it the capital of the Roman Empire. Paul's group stayed only for a week. Not wanting their last night in town to end, they hung out together late into the night (Acts 20).

ANOTHER UPPER ROOM

Luke records others who were on this trip. The most notable name on the list is Timothy, Paul's protégé, who became like a son to him. Timothy is mentioned a couple of chapters earlier in Acts 16:1, and he's the first second-generation Christian mentioned in the New Testament. The other men were close companions of Paul who carried his most personal messages and endured persecution alongside him. Paul and his entourage spent that evening in the upstairs room of a house that belonged to one of the members of the local church.

Houses weren't the biggest to begin with, but gatherings in an upper room such as the one described here would have kept everyone especially snug. The room was cramped and hot, but also familiar, and they didn't have to hide as was the case in so many other places. Local believers were eager to attend this particular gathering for a couple of reasons.

First, Paul had become a bit of a celebrity. This was his second trip to Troas, and word of his ministry had been well-publicized. Not only did he preach with authority, he was one of the people who had seen the risen Jesus. Time and time again, people asked him about it. At the time of this meeting, it had been a little more than twenty years since the resurrection of Jesus. Younger believers were awestruck by the presence of a seasoned leader like Paul who had survived everything from shipwrecks to mobs that wanted to rip him apart limb by limb.

Another reason these disciples flocked to the upper room to be with Paul was to learn from his leadership. Paul was a significant leader, and these disciples learned much of their content and style from him. They wouldn't be able to Skype him in a few weeks when they had questions about the tough objections and persecution coming at them. They wanted to absorb as much training and encouragement as Paul was willing to offer.

The room was warming up and not just because of body heat. The assembled guests had also eaten dinner, and they probably cooked the food in an earthen oven or open hearth on the bottom floor. So you have a stuffy house filled with stuffed people after a big meal. On top of that, it's a naturally warm climate. Plus, it's nighttime, so a bunch of lamps were lit. The smell of those wicker fumes filled every space in the room. Who can blame a young man named Eutychus for getting tired as Paul talked late into the night?

BEST SEAT IN THE HOUSE?

Ever dream you're falling? Hopefully you woke up and found yourself in bed. Or on a couch. Or at least somewhere other than midair. Eutychus had that same dream, except he really was falling.

Some call Eutychus the patron saint of people who sleep in church. Anyone who has ever nodded off in church or a classroom can relate. Luke says that Paul talked on and on. A lot of us have fought against heavier-than-realistically-possible eyelids in hard-backed pews as a preacher droned on and on. We'll never know for sure, but I'm pretty confident there's a class in seminaries about how to make people think you're wrapping a sermon up even though you're really just going to say "in conclusion" a bunch of times. Not that I've ever gotten nailed for the fake ending move a lot when speaking in front of groups.

The lifeblood of a church is in its substance, not its style. Calling a church lifeless is just another way of saying it's dead. If that's the case, then the message must be hollow, powerless. God isn't boring. Nobody ever falls asleep from boredom during real encounters with the maker of the universe. Yet sometimes we end up doing faith in ways that are painfully dull. However, sometimes we are lifeless, dead, and it really doesn't matter where we go to find meaning. Anyway, good speaker or not, it's never a good idea to fall asleep while sitting on a window ledge three stories up.

Luke calls Eutychus a neanias (neh-ah-ni-as), which indicates that he was an adult in his prime, a twenty- or thirty-something in today's language. He may have been a servant. Either way, he likely woke early and worked hard. So he wasn't necessarily just being lazy or ignorant. In fact, he might have gone to that window for some fresh air, doing his best to stay awake. In any case, no one else paid much attention to him as Paul captivated the room.

I've taught at multiple colleges and seen plenty of sleeping students. In some speaking venues I've even had family members fall asleep on me! It really doesn't bother me. But I like to have some fun when my younger students fall asleep, especially those who obviously partied too hard the night before or stayed up all night playing video games. I used to stack Starburst on sleepers to see how many I could get before they woke up. They look pretty funny when they do, all confused as to why everyone's laughing at them as candy rains from their clothing. We can have fun with sleepers like Eutychus, but dozing off certainly doesn't warrant death.

CHURCH OF THE MAGIC EYE

A few years ago, those Magic Eye pictures were all the rage. If you stared at a page of jumbled colors long enough, you were supposed to be able to make out some hidden 3-D object that only became apparent after your mind unlocked the secret. To this day I have never successfully seen one of those stupid hidden images. I guess I don't have magic eyes. I hate those pictures.[2]

Christian spirituality is sometimes like those hidden pictures. People in churches have different perspectives on what they're looking at. Sometimes we have to wonder if we're all even looking at the same thing. For me, going to church used to be like looking

---

2. Not that I'm bitter or anything.

at a Magic Eye picture. I thought that there might be something good to see, and other people seemed to really love what they were experiencing, but I was just looking at a jumbled mess. I felt disconnected. Why were the speakers so moved? Why did those people put their hands in the air during songs? Why would a church plan an event when football was on at the same time? Church was often a chore, more of an obligation than anything I actually wanted to be a part of. It wasn't working. I got frustrated. Church wasn't a great experience, just something I tried that didn't really work.

On many Sundays in my life, I was one of the zombievangelicals—those empty, shambling masses that are symptomatic of faith decay. Unfortunately, many modern churches are filled with zombie worshipers who moan and shuffle through the motions like that. I could barely stay awake through the service but came to full life right after the service in anticipation of something fun like a barbecue and pool party or the football game of the day. Some mornings I don't think much about God yet have no trouble burning time on the internet. I don't believe that God sits on a cloud with a clipboard waiting to send us to detention, but I often think about how little sense some of my actions make based on what I say I believe. For example, if I'm right about God then I don't even have my next breath without God's divine blessing. How do we forget about someone like that?

What we see in regard to our purpose, problems, and pain depends on where we place our focus. The simplest way to break this down is to say that we can either focus on ourselves most or on someone else. If we focus on ourselves, then our purpose remains uncertain, our problems continue to confuse us, and our pain is never properly dealt with. Only in God do we find clarity of purpose, answers to our problems, and healing for whatever hurts.

Going to church can be different. Our view of God changes over the years, and we can find churches where the people and teaching are real. Authenticity really matters. We can all sniff out fakeness in the twenty-first century because our culture is defined by it, right down to reality TV, an entertainment train wreck we just can't stop craning our necks to watch. Mostly we just like to see if other people are more screwed up than we are. We're a cynical bunch, which is why the last thing anyone wants to hear, especially in church, is how perfect someone thinks he or she is. If there's ever a place to be real, it's within the church. Community like that—like the kind Paul found in Troas—has to be based on authentic relationships. We want our pastors to tell us that he's not perfect because life isn't easy. We shouldn't act like a different person for one hour on Sunday. (Sometimes I get emotional and choked up and have to pretend that something's in my eye so other people won't realize I'm not as cool as everyone surely thinks I am.) We can just be ourselves and don't have to pretend to have it all together. Finding an environment like that is key to spiritual vitality.

Like all my friends who one by one were always able to finally see the stupid magic dolphin or whatever was in those Magic Eye pictures, we can shift our vision to really see God. The great thing about that breakthrough is that even when something distorts our view of God now, we've had those glimpses of something way bigger than us that is real. God is there even if we don't always see him as clearly as we want. It's a lot like Lazarus coming out of his tomb. He heard the voice of Jesus and knew his Savior was out there even though his eyes were covered with those grave clothes as he hobbled out of his tomb.

THE FALL OF A STUDENT

Eutychus fell asleep on that window ledge and went over the edge. I wonder what thoughts raced through his mind in those final moments. His life must have flashed before his eyes, but mostly he probably had some variation of this thought: *How could I have been so stupid!* He was trapped in a nightmare, and there was no escape as he hung there in the air, halfway between this world and the next.

The Message uses the word "toppled" to describe how he fell. We all know what it's like to lose control of our senses while nodding off. Ever try to catch yourself as you start to fall asleep only to realize you're safely planted on a couch? It's so embarrassing when that happens in the middle of a crowded room, especially if you do the whole snore-snort-head snap like I do. Eutychus went from disorientation to terrifying awareness in nanoseconds and tried to grasp at anything he could find to save him. He couldn't get a grip on anything.

That's how our lives look when we lose focus and fall asleep at the proverbial switch guiding our lives. By the time we realize how much trouble we're in—relationship disasters, financial crises, unexpected pregnancies—it's too late. The awareness of how far out of control we are can be terrifying. Once things get that bad, it's hard to even get a grip on the situation and, by extension, our lives.

We fall in a variety of ways but especially for lies. We're all susceptible to deception. Like zombies, the people who mess us up the most usually go for the brain. Lies can derail morality and undermine faith. And they are everywhere, not just in the words people use. Our society is filled with deception: from the misleading appearance of success to things we call problems from inside our comfortable bubbles.

Perhaps the biggest lie of all is that there is no such thing as absolute truth. If that's the case, then we're all free to create whatever standard of right and wrong we want. If it feels good, do it. But the problem with such a worldview is that nothing ultimately matters because meaning is always rooted in truth. Nothing would be real in a world without absolutes. The devil is called the father of lies for a reason. To call truth relative is to take aim at the very heart of God.

In an earlier chapter, I mentioned that I like Alexander Hamilton (and even have a piece of his hair). His short lifetime included both fantastic success and spectacular failure, but in the end, he knew what he believed in. He once said, "Those who stand for nothing will fall for anything." That's the danger of being hollow. It's hard to go through life without falling, even when we stand on a solid foundation of truth. Going through life without any particular kind of belief is like taking a nap on an open third-story window ledge. Something bad is bound to happen.

CAN'T HAVE A FUNERAL WITHOUT A BODY

What would some of these biblical events have looked like if there had been a local nightly news broadcast or, even worse, cable news in the first century? In the case of Eutychus, you know that Fox News and CNN would have instantly prepared headline graphics with phrases like "Out on a Ledge" or "Third-story Sleeper" while concerned-looking reporters would implement all the tools of their training, which consist of furrowing their eyebrows in concern and repeating other people's statements back to them in the form of a question.[3]

REPORTER: Now witnesses say that the young man fell from that third-story window sometime after midnight during a gathering of members of a religious sect known as The Way. I'm here with Luke, one of the men who was in that room at the time of the accident. Can you tell us what happened?

LUKE: Well, he fell out of that window and landed right here. When they picked him up, he was dead. But Paul—

REPORTER: Wait a second, how do you know he was dead?

LUKE: Because I'm a doctor, man, not an ignorant bystander.

REPORTER: I see. Go on.

---

3. Not that I'm critical of television news or anything.

LUKE: Like I was saying. Paul, he's our leader, went down, stretched himself out on the victim just like Elijah and Elisha did in the old days. Ancient CPR, you know? We were all afraid, but Paul was like "Don't worry. He's still alive." All of a sudden the dead guy's chest began rising and falling. I checked his pulse and there it was again! It was crazy.

REPORTER: I'll say. Where is the young man now?

LUKE: Oh, he's sleeping.

REPORTER: And there's no concern about his condition? Is he stable?

LUKE: Sleeping like a baby. We're talking about a miracle here, pal. It's not like God rescues people from death to only bring them halfway.

REPORTER: That's quite a story. Where's Paul now? Can we speak with him?

LUKE: He went back to the service. They're having communion now. Matter of fact, I gotta get up there to celebrate with them.

REPORTER: What's communion?

After that, the networks would have a couple of resurrection experts who disagree with each other come on the show to clarify the story by screaming at each other, even though neither one of them had any actual connection to the event.

I guess what I'm trying to say is that miraculous events of this magnitude probably weren't much easier to explain in the first century than they are now. Also, cable news makes me want to throw my television out of a third-story window.

Luke made a great witness, by the way. He alone recorded the first resurrection in Nain and was present for this last such miracle recorded in the New Testament. In fact, he was the only one to record five of the six individual cases of dead people being brought back to life. Lazarus's resuscitation was the only one he didn't chronicle.

THE SCARS REMAIN

Paul had a lot going on. He was backtracking all over Asia because people wanted to capture and kill him. He knew that he had to go to Jerusalem even though it meant big trouble, and all his friends warned against the trip. He was also under the emotional strain of never seeing many of his friends again. We see this in the very next section in Acts, after his encounter with Eutychus. It features a powerful good-bye to the leaders of the church at Ephesus. They all ended up weeping, embracing, and praying on the beach before Paul headed off to what would be his eventual execution. And right in the middle of all of these tumultuous events, a tragic accident kills one of the young believers in Troas while he was speaking. It's a good thing Paul wasn't the type to give in to despair every time something went wrong.

Before God confronted Paul on the road to Damascus with a cosmic wake-up call, he spent his life persecuting Christians. The first high-profile case in which Paul, then called Saul, is introduced is at the stoning of Stephen—the first recorded Christian martyr. Luke described the execution in Acts 7. It's hard to overstate the brutality of being stoned to death, to be hit in the face or have your collarbone snapped by a large rock. Barbaric.

Throughout that lynching, Paul watched and signaled approval. He looked into the face of Stephen as the murderous mob carried on. Unless God graciously blocked out those terrible memories, Paul spent the rest of his life with that picture of innocent Stephen's face seared into his mind. Maybe in some way Paul was doubly blessed when God used him to bring Eutychus back to life, like God allowed Paul to resuscitate another man so he could experience some kind of balance for the death he ordained.

After Paul revived Eutychus, the group found a place to lay him until morning and went back to their gathering, where they shared communion. Once again, food played a major part during a night of tragedy and the miraculous. They no doubt talked about what had just happened. A few of the people in that room had seen some amazing things take place over the previous couple of years. Someone in the room probably pointed out the irony that the name Eutychus means "fortunate." He had himself quite a night.

As far as we can tell, he suffered the most violent death of all the resuscitated New Testament people.[4] Luke doesn't describe any physical trauma such as blood or broken bones, but falling out of a third-floor window is going to do some damage.

One of my favorite bands, Disciple, has a song called "Scars Remain." The song describes the scars we carry through life and how they remind us of painful experiences. But when we look at Christ, we see that he also has scars that match ours. It's a beautiful

---

4. Not counting the resurrected Jesus, of course.

picture. Jesus suffered such a violent death, but his body carried the scars that proved the completeness of his work on earth. If Eutychus was left physically scarred after his death that night, he could always look at those marks and remember how God brought him from death to life.

Our scars all tell stories. My right arm reminds me of the worst bike wreck I ever experienced. My left side reminds me of the time my friend's dog bit me. My forehead features a little crease from where I got stitches as a four-year-old after smashing my head on the corner of an end table because my sister was chasing me.

Emotional scars work the same way. Our hearts are seared with painful memories of things that have happened to us. Each time we experience pain, the restoration process brings us back a little more calloused, a little tougher. The strangest things can trigger these painful scars to reopen like a healing wound. A certain song on the radio or perfume on some random person or a sudden flash-back. Sometimes we cringe or feel physically ill at the memory, but we try to remember that what we're recalling is just another example of something painful that we've made it through. We're restored even though the scars remain. They're a sign of healing.

DEATH IN THE DARKNESS

The moral of this story could be that it's better to sit on the floor than in a window if you think you'll fall asleep during church. OK, so there's more to it than that. The story of Eutychus shows that God can act in an incredible way during tragedies and that divine presence brings people closer to each other.

Paul and his friends stayed up through the night because he was leaving in the morning. They loved one another and didn't want their fleeting time together to end. We don't need a building with a steeple to enter into community. Living rooms, dorm rooms, and garages make fine settings for coming together in spiritual unity. Accountability and encouragement are critical for every one of us, and those things only come from people who care about us and with whom we can get real. We need to get connected somewhere whether we've found a church that feels like home or not.

It's not all peaches and cream, though. Just like the creation of a beautiful song, community includes discord as well as harmony. Groups fight. Churches split. Denominations feud. Jesus knew we would struggle to stay united and even mentioned future believers in his final group prayer. "I am praying not only for these disciples but also for all who will ever believe in me because of their testimony. My prayer for all of them is that they will be one, just as you and I are one, Father" (John 17:20-21 NLT). Sometimes we get burned by becoming vulnerable enough to trust a group of people. But that just means we need to keep searching for the right community. We were not made to be cut off from everyone.

In the realm of the living dead, zombies move in hordes. They are unknowingly cliquish, and even though they're slow and clumsy, their power is in their numbers. Vampires, on the other hand, are the loners of the undead world (despite the occasional coven here and there), highly independent and usually enamored with their power. It's easy to take on those two roles in our faith. Most of the time, we move in cliques like zombies yet do the hardest parts of life and faith alone like vampires. We know a lot of people on a superficial level but don't really have deep, meaningful connections with them. I don't think we should run around blabbing our deepest secrets to everyone we meet. That's not wise. But we should focus on that delicate balance between being too strongly influenced by others and never letting anybody get close to us.

We need to be connected because isolation kills. Sometimes literally.

It probably sounds like a provocative thing to say, but we constantly see tragedies occur in society with individuals who were completely alone for far too long. We can hear the news reports now. "Neighbors say that the suspect mostly kept to himself." Now, not all who are alone are dangers to themselves or others. Nor is isolation always bad. Sometimes it's necessary. Jesus showed as much when he went solo into the desert. But prolonged isolation is not healthy. We begin to believe our lies after a while. The most dangerous self-deceptions are wrapped in pain and lead to despair.

Lies about our worthlessness are never louder than when we're all alone. A staggering study shows that 50 percent of college students had thought about suicide, 15 percent had seriously considered it, and 5 percent had attempted it.[5] Reading those numbers

5. The 2008 article is called "Half of College Students Consider Suicide" and can be found at www.msnbc.msn.com/id/26272639/ns/health-mental_half-college-students-consider-suicide/.

is like getting punched in the gut. Staring at college classrooms all the time makes it impossible to forget those numbers. A couple of students even confided in me about their struggles and the life-and-death thoughts that went along with them. It's painful to know that even one person has considered suicide, no matter how fleeting a thought it might be. The possibility that half of the students in one of my classrooms has been in that dark place is impossible to comprehend. One of the reasons my brain goes into spasms when people say that there are no absolutes—besides the fact that the statement eats itself—is that when we lose truth, we lose ultimate meaning and purpose.

Without anyone else around we can become delusional, losing contact with reality as we lose contact with others. Everyone struggles with meaninglessness to a certain extent at some point. Those feelings grow strongest in isolation just as bacteria grow best in darkness, away from sunlight and its purifying ultraviolet rays.

Remember those zombie ants? The infected creatures do something that had researchers baffled for some time. After stumbling away from their colonies, all the doomed ants arrive at their graveyard and bite down on a leaf vein at the same time. How could these insects, scattered all over the rain forest, commit such a specific act with such synchronization? The best theory is that the temperature and light of midday draw the ants to a specific spot where they clamp down. But they don't die until sunset. The zombie fungus drives them toward an ideal location but doesn't kill its host until nightfall because then it is guaranteed a long, cold night during which to burst out of the ant's head. A short while later, it releases those deadly spores all over the area to ensure that this first victim leads to many others.

Thoughts and emotions that poison our minds and hearts always flourish most during long, cold nights of isolation. We must guard against lies that say life is pointless, we're not worth anything, and no one cares. Life is a gift; we each have a purpose, and God cares so much that he was willing to die to prove it. If we're surrounded by people who make us feel worthless, then perhaps it's time to get away from them. At the very least know that there are people out there who truly care.

We were not made to be alone. God said as much after creating the first human (Genesis 2:18). We need the light of others to encourage us and to provide a reality check against shortsighted perspectives. A solid community of believers can be there for us in our darkest moments. Accountability works both ways, though, and we should lift up those around us, always looking out for the people God places in our path. We also need to constantly keep our minds in check, just like those zombie ants. Eutychus is often criticized for falling asleep, but he was exactly where he should've been—surrounded by a community who loved him, while focusing on God.

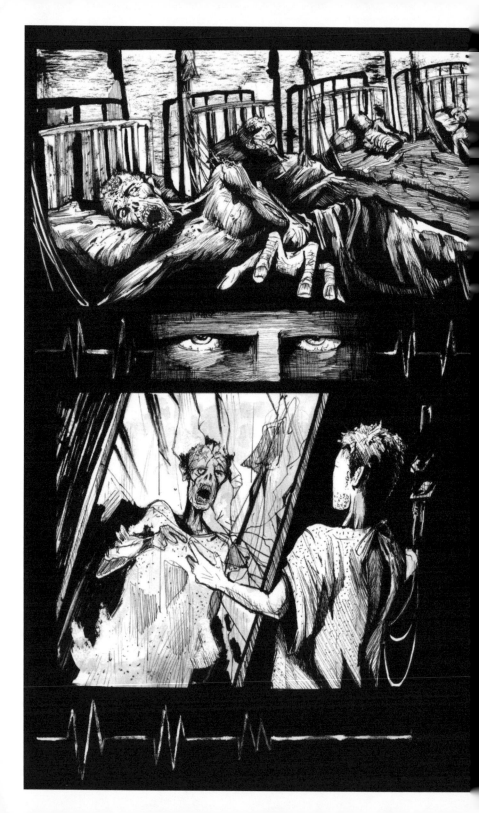

CHAPTER 11

THE DEAD LIVE

I am still in the land of the dying; I shall be in the land of the living soon.

—John Newton

Ghost hunters believe that Gettysburg, Pennsylvania, is one of the most haunted places in the world. The town was the site of the pivotal battle during the American Civil War; more men fought and died at Gettysburg during the first three days of July 1863 than in any other battle in American history. The casualty figures topped fifty thousand. The Confederates had five thousand casualties in one hour alone during the epic failure known as Pickett's Charge. Locals tell legends about tortured souls who cry out from the ground, like the blood of Abel shed by his brother Cain.

The men who died there were not on their way to Gettysburg,

but that's where they encountered the enemy. That's where they fell and died. Those men, many of them barely more than boys, were just trying to make their way through the battle, a grueling journey where fear and obstacles appeared in their path every day. Just like that, a little town became a morgue. A random field became a cemetery. The ground became hallowed. Local leaders asked President Abraham Lincoln to make a personal visit and give a speech to consecrate the place of remembrance.

The president only spoke for a couple of minutes, and many of the twenty thousand people in attendance were unable to hear him, but his poetic address is considered one of the most beautiful and lasting in history. Lincoln said that mere words meant nothing. Dedicating ourselves to "the unfinished work . . . a great task remaining before us" was all that mattered. Our devotion should be increased by remembering the sacrifices of those who went before us so that we could experience "a new birth of freedom" with God's help.

When Lincoln finished his speech, the assembled statesmen, soldiers, and spectators were silent. Lincoln thought he had disappointed everybody, but their silence signaled stunned reflection as the impact of what had happened sunk into their hearts and minds, just as the blood of those boys had soaked into the hallowed soil beneath their feet.

LINCOLN AND THE UNDEAD

Lincoln will never die. His legacy lives on through his words and deeds, and he remains a compelling figure more than two centuries after his birth. His whole life was struggle. He lived in a time when millions of his fellow humans were enslaved. He oversaw a war to end that evil institution and to preserve the unity of the country he loved and led. He felt the weight of reports day after day as more than six hundred thousand soldiers died on his watch. And he endured the deaths of two of his four sons in the years before his own life was cut short by assassin John Wilkes Booth in 1865. The bullet that took Lincoln's life prevented him from watching a third son die a few years later.

With such a tragic and high-profile life, it's no wonder that Lincoln's faith continues to spark discussion. Author Seth Grahame-Smith fictionalized the legendary president as a stalker of the undead in a well-written novel called *Abraham Lincoln: Vampire Hunter*. It's fun to imagine our nation's sixteenth president taking out slave-owning vampires with a throwing axe; good versus evil at its finest.

When I was a graduate assistant, our history department organized a class to be held for one week in Washington D.C. I had heard about a book in the private attic of Ford's Theater rumored to include a letter written by Lincoln about his spiritual beliefs. I phoned ahead and received special permission to visit the archives on the top floor beyond the velvet rope near the building's entrance.

I ducked away from a lunch with some friends at the Lincoln Waffle Shop across the street from the theater to begin my investigation. I didn't tell anyone what I was doing because I didn't know how to explain that it somehow mattered to me whether or not Abraham Lincoln had believed the same things about Jesus that I thought I did. As strange as it sounds, I remember asking my mom when I was a little boy if Lincoln had gone to heaven or not. Yes, I've always been a history dork, but I have no idea why I worried about the eternal fate of a dead president when I was only five years old.

With the help of a kind historian, I found the letter. Well into the Civil War, a pastor from Lincoln's hometown of Springfield, Illinois, wanted to know what the president thought of Jesus; if he loved him. I thumbed through the crisp pages of that old volume and found Lincoln's reply. The president said that he didn't consider himself a Christian when he arrived at the White House or when his eleven-year-old son Willie died. But, Lincoln wrote, he committed his life to Christ after arriving at Gettysburg in 1863 and seeing the graves of thousands upon thousands of fallen soldiers.

If that letter is accurate, then Gettysburg doesn't just commemorate the death of thousands; it also marks the spot where at least one man found ultimate life.

How did Lincoln come to see God so clearly amid so much carnage, to see beauty in all that pain? The weight of death and war must have been crushing him, yet he discovered in that moment a loving God willing and able to remove painful burdens. How personal the "new birth of freedom" that he spoke about in the Gettysburg Address must have been for him. Could it be that Lincoln found personal liberation from the bondage of human nature and the wrongness we all know even as he sought to liberate humankind from a different kind of slavery? Crossing from spiritual death to life is about finding freedom. If this account is true, it sounds like the Great Emancipator realized his own freedom as he granted the same to so many others.

SUPERMAN

I loved Superman when I was a kid. I had the pajamas, the makeshift cape, and possibly even the underwear.[1] Superheroes have changed a lot over the years. Modern audiences like their heroes to be conflicted about morality. We connect with protagonists who haven't got it all figured out. But Superman fought for truth and justice and always did what was right. When Superman told Lois Lane that you should never lie, it affected me deeply. I did not want to let him down.

When I saw *Superman II*, I was shocked. The basic plot is that Superman is too disconnected from regular humans, especially Lois Lane, whom he really loves, so he overdoses on some bad kryptonite in order to give away his superpowers and become just a regular guy. Reality sets in after he gets socked in the face by some trucker jerk and sees his own blood. The unthinkable happened: Superman was a wimp. A nasty enemy shows up to take control of everything, and Superman is powerless to do anything about it. Thankfully, one last supernatural moment enables him to regain his invincibility, and he takes out the bad guys just when they thought they had won.

---

1. OK, so I definitely had the underwear.

As kids, we would never understand why Superman would give up his powers. His motivation wouldn't make any sense until we got a little older. Then we start to understand the power of love and how it can drive someone to do something so irrational that they would even be willing to die. We'll never fully comprehend the love of God, but that picture of Superman helps. The Almighty Creator of the universe became a regular guy for love.

BE MORE LIKE THE PROSTITUTE

Often we forget how much God so loved the world and only worry about how much he hated sin. Maybe it's not fashionable to use a word like *sin*. But when something is screwed up on this planet, it has everything to do with humans. We're not perfect. Call it what you will, but the word *sin* helps express the reality of our imperfect nature. We understand sin really well, like, intimately. So it's tough for us when churches push ideas about good stuff and bad stuff and how the right balance adds up to God. It's an unwinnable equation that we create. (And since we're imperfect then it's no wonder that our self-made religious systems are flawed as well.)

In between the story of the widow at Nain and the account of Jairus's daughter, Luke tells another tale (Luke 7:36-50). One of the Pharisees invited Jesus over for dinner. As they reclined at the table, a "sinful woman" showed up. Her tears fell on Jesus' feet, watery confessions splashing the spot that would soon be pierced by a metal spike. She wiped those tears with her hair, kissed his feet, and poured costly perfume on them. Jesus thought it was beautiful. The Pharisee thought it was disgusting.

See, the Pharisee types fall into the trap of simplifying God into some second-grade concept of good versus bad. If we're living in a way we know to be wrong, then God doesn't love us because of our bad behavior. If we believe we're doing everything right, then God loves us because we're such a good person or something. Completely untrue.

Meanwhile, Jesus wonders why the prostitute at his feet is the only person in a room full of religious leaders and his "followers" who gets it. There's something they never told us in Sunday school: Be more like the prostitute. But the woman at Jesus' feet understood that the antidote to spiritual death, being lifeless inside, isn't just to do more things right.

Many of us think that God will be pleased if we avoid doing all the "bad" things that are out there. Yet we can exhibit a lot of good behavior and still not really care about what God cares about or even know who he is. If there's any lie more dangerous than "You're worthless" it's one that tells us we are so good that we don't need God. Getting it right is more about who we serve than what we do. The solution is to see God clearly because everything else pales in comparison to the reality of who he is. How do we see God more clearly?

Paul had it right when he said Jesus is "the visible image of the invisible God" (Colossians 1:15 NLT). So what kinds of clues can we get about God by looking at the way Jesus lived? For starters, he spent a lot more time showing people what was good rather than wasting time bashing people for being so bad. He didn't have to tell most people that their actions were wrong because they knew his were so right. People who had genuine encounters with him weren't the same afterward. They still faced struggles, had miserable days, and dealt with tragedy, but they found their hope and strength in the riches of his grace rather than in the bankruptcy of their own powerlessness. As Ravi Zacharias often says, Jesus didn't come to make bad people good. He came to make dead people live.

FAITH OF THE LIVING DEAD

God should also be visible through his representatives on earth. The church is called the body of Christ because it's meant to be the hands and feet that carry out the work of heaven. Sadly, we have some issues in this department. The word *Christian* carries some stigma because we've hurt people. One of the toughest objections we ever face is when people say, "If God is so great and Jesus changes lives then how come his followers _____?" A lot of different criticisms—act like jerks, hypocrites, or miserable, unchanged people for starters—get plugged into that blank. Christians have to accept some level of blame for how many people view God. My friend Knox started a website called The My Bad Project as a forum for people who are willing to point out ways we've blown it as ambassadors for God. As Knox says, "Sometimes apologizing is better than evangelizing."

People might reject God or Christianity or even mock Jesus, but no one actually has any reason to find fault in how he lived. His whole life was love. He stood against hypocrisy and cared for the neediest people in the world. If we all imitated him, the world's problems would be over. But we don't.

The truth of the matter is that a lot of us, churchgoers and skeptics alike, just don't think Jesus is that special. We might believe to a certain extent, but most of our physical needs are already met and life rolls on. There's still plenty of stuff we want, though, so we stay busy trying to track it all down. Maybe we check in with God now and again when we get some free time, but that's about it. After all, God is invisible. Final exams and bills and crying children are not. We put up with that stuff because we believe in a good career, nice house, or loving family. All of those things are nice, but when they fail to deliver the ultimate satisfaction we were hoping for, we feel dead inside.

Most of us would like to rearrange our priorities, but reality gets in the way. The challenges we all face, and resulting spiritual ignorance, are nothing new. Written a couple thousand years ago, the last book of the Bible records a divine critique against the church in a place called Sardis: "I know all the things you do, and that you have a reputation for being alive—but you are dead" (Revelation 3:1 NLT). Ouch. We can relate. Many of us have a good reputation as spiritual people while actually being dead inside. We can only hide our grave clothes for so long before we start to stinketh.

Somewhere along the line a lot of us got this idea that

spiritual death meant rejecting God or worshiping Satan or something. At the same time, we generated our divine to-do lists. We go through the motions and check off our spiritual boxes—punching in on Sunday, tossing a couple of bucks in the offering plate, sporting a Jesus-y bumper sticker—so we're safe. We turn faith into housekeeping for the soul. Just tidy up the obvious stuff when people are around and sweep the tricky bits under the rug.

Call it whatever kind of faith you want—dead, hollow, empty—I had it. I said I believed in certain things but nothing I did really lined up with what I was telling myself and others. I practiced the faith of the living dead in which believers are a lot like zombies: human shells more dead than alive inside. The undead don't exactly draw others in. Spiritual death isn't pretty.

Positive changes begin when we finally start to realize who God actually is rather than many of the misconceptions we carry around. God and reality come together. The world begins spinning with the power of that endless revelation. Earth-shaking stuff. Then he breathes life into us in a way we have never encountered. When we move out of the darkness and toward him, the light will hurt our eyes. It might not be pretty, but there we are. Alive. We hear an unfamiliar heartbeat and realize that the pulse isn't even coming from inside of us. It's the heartbeat of God, and we're hearing it for the first time.

It's much better to try to explain what God means to me rather than to pretend that I'm better than anyone or that I somehow have an inside connection with the Almighty. That's the kind of spiritual elitism that makes folks on the receiving end of judgmental snobbery become bitter and resentful. God's the one who is better, not me. We have a lot of work to do if he's going to be clearly seen through his representatives on earth.

THE STRUGGLE

Many of us are too overwhelmed by finitude to give infinity much thought. In other words, what about right now? How do we come back from spiritual death now?

It's tough to stay focused on things that matter. We easily get sidetracked by the view of success and happiness that most people hold. Society can really screw us up. A lot. Many of the choking weeds of spiritual death are rooted in the misdirected attitudes of culture. As kids, people ask us what we'll be when we grow up, but *who* we'll be is more important. As adults, our roles are defined every time we meet someone new. "So what do you do?" we ask each other, still focusing on what we produce or make rather than how we live. A simple phrase like "be somebody" can even be a subtle killer. It's tough enough to be the person we are supposed to be without trying to be who everyone else wants us to be. The preoccupation with how we measure up in the view of everyone around us is often overwhelming. The more we look at what others have, the less we consider what God has given us. The more we think about ourselves, the less we think about God. Spiritual death and selfishness like to share lusty beds in the seedy part of our brains.

We often talk about "finding ourselves" as if self-discovery is the key that unlocks the door to happiness. I looked for myself for a long time and tried all kinds of things that I thought might make me complete. Finding myself wasn't very helpful. In fact, the more I got to know myself, the more trouble I got into. And maybe self-discovery has been a key part of improving life for many people. Personally, I needed less of myself and more of something greater than me.

History is filled with people who had everything yet felt unfulfilled. We believe our lives will be better when we get to the next step—whether it's finding a spouse, having a baby, getting a promotion, accruing massive wealth, getting plastic surgery, or whatever. But what happens when we have everything and still wake up feeling empty? At that point, there's nothing left to search after in hopes of finding happiness. Maybe delusion is the ultimate weapon. Without it, we are stripped bare.

The life of faith is a power struggle. Some people give control of their lives to God; others don't. Many people ultimately refuse to turn to God because that response requires a forfeiture of control. The closer we move to him, the more we have to acknowledge our lack of power. But such recognition is key to finding ourselves. The illumination is painful, as we see ourselves clearly, so a lot of us choose to skip the whole process.

We live in an age of anxiety. Everyone is under so much pressure. Psychiatrists and psychologists spend endless hours attempting to calm anxious souls. The problem is universal, not just limited to people who lack faith. Perhaps all this tension, fear, and panic are a result of attempting to control everything so much.

Marcus Goodyear—senior editor of *The High Calling* webzine—says that "What we fear teaches us a lot about what we worship."[2] If you don't think about God much, then the idea of worship probably isn't something that takes up too much of your brainpower. But we all worship something. Another word for worship is adoration. In other words, what do you long for? What do you think about? We want our hearts to be worshipful toward God as a way of life, but all that visible stuff always gets in the way. Distractions kill worship. Sometimes I get text messages when I'm trying to pray. I know I shouldn't want to look at my phone since I'm communing with the Almighty Creator of the universe and everything, but what if I miss a really important Twitter update? I feel pathetic. It's like saying, "Hold on a sec God. I have another call."

If God appeared right in front of me, I wouldn't be worried about whether or not I got any new e-mails. I'd probably be speechless. I would definitely fall flat on my face. But since God doesn't show up like that these days—at least not in Pennsylvania as far as I can tell—I guess "out of sight out of mind" often trumps worship. But God did show up in the form of Jesus, someone we could connect with and understand without passing out from fear. But apparently, the more approachable God becomes, the less likely it is that people will worship him.

There's a lot we don't know about the life of Jesus, especially his family life. Like how many funerals did Jesus go to? We can be pretty certain that he buried his earthly father, Joseph. That had

2. Marcus Goodyear, "Zombies for the Love of God," www.thehigh calling.org/7649/zombies-for-the-love-of-god.

to be tough, especially watching his mother, Mary, mourn the loss of her husband. Jesus' family probably put some pressure on him when loved ones became ill, too, but even Jesus had to experience the tension between doing what was possible and what God wanted. Each time Jesus watched someone die, his human side felt the emotion of loss while the divine part saw the consequence of sin.

We do know that for a long time his brother James did not believe in Jesus' divinity. We probably would have snapped at Jesus if he was our older brother and our dad or someone we cared about was sick. We might have even yelled at him. "Why won't you do something? Don't you understand?" Ironically, we would be saying that to the only person who did understand. He probably would be really nice to us even though we were acting like jerks, and for sure he'd be thinking about the role of his own death. That was the bottom line for him. Creation was perfect until sin hit the fan because of man. The result is death. God hates death. The only way to defeat sin was through resurrection by a different man.

A lot of us think about sin as the bad things people do rather than its more meaningful definition as a condition of separation from God. Sin is a disease, like your typical zombie virus. Every human catches it, and the condition is terminal. God loves us and hates to see us die, both physically and spiritually.

Yet unlike those plagues that wipe out humanity in the movies, this disease is curable. The antidote is the cross, so we're offered a trade. We can nail our death—the sin shell—to the cross in exchange for life. The greatest miracle ever is the work of redeeming us from spiritual death. The feeling of being freed from heavy burdens is indescribable. It's like when waking up from a nightmare and being filled with relief. Even though not consciously aware of the desperation as you slept, you subconsciously knew that something about you was terribly wrong, and you're so glad when you snap out of it. Paul said, "The hour has come for you to wake up from your slumber" (Romans 13:11).

THE DEATH OF DEATH

Vampires, zombies, ghosts, and undead creatures appeal to us because eternity has been set in our hearts. Our limited minds aren't able to comprehend infinity, yet humankind has long been obsessed with immortality. We feel that there's something beyond this existence. A person's soul, spirit, essence, or whatever we want to call it must live forever.

In all our speculation we've created fictional scenarios in which life beyond the grave happens right here on earth. It's part of what makes creatures of the night so interesting. In some ways, visions of undead hordes aren't too far from what the Bible predicts. That's what resurrection is, after all. Dead people will come back to life. If Scripture is accurate, then we are all getting a seriously extreme makeover for eternity—a version of our bodies that can never be destroyed.

Paul said the perishable will become imperishable. First-century believers like the Corinthians were already asking him how such a thing could be possible. "How are the dead raised?" they wondered. "With what kind of body will they come?" It's like they were saying, "How could this possibly work? What would a corpse look like if it was pulled from the grave? Are you nuts?!"[3] Even New Testament listeners in places like Corinth envisioned grim, zombielike bodies.

Paul responded by pointing out the laws of nature. Flowers and plants are not put in the ground. Seeds are. They look nothing like that which they yield but must first be put in the ground. The death of those seeds leads to new life and beauty. He described how even in our current understanding we know there are heavenly bodies like the sun, moon, and stars that we can see with our earthly bodies. We can understand that a gap exists between these realms, but transformation must occur in order to bridge it.

If we're honest, most of us have thought about ways we would like to change our body. We dream about bodies that are not only perfect but also immune to sickness—bodies that can never die because death will be dead. Christ's work on the cross means we don't even have to fear death. Paul knew it when he asked, "Where, O death, is your victory? / Where, O death, is your sting?" (1 Corinthians 15:55). The sting of death is sin, and God nailed it to the cross to make a spectacle of it.

Out of all the crazy stories in this book, Jesus is the only one who raised *himself* from the dead. Everyone else was just resuscitated. They came back to life for a while but still had to die again. A resurrected person is *immortal*. Imagine what it will be like to have a physical body and yet never have to fear death. Without death to fear we are truly free to live.

---

3. Paul's breakdown of these questions is in 1 Corinthians 15.

THE FINISH LINE

Our spiritual journey is like *The Wizard of Oz* and that yellow brick road. Dorothy struggles to stay on the path even though it's clearly defined. Somebody laid that foundation and many others had followed the shiny trail to the Emerald City. Why is it so difficult to stay on track? The challenges never stop. An enemy launches attacks.

Dorothy finds faithful companions along the way, but they are as much restricted by one another's weaknesses as they are strengthened by one another's encouragement. And when they finally catch sight of their glorious destination and believe the worst is over, they fall victim to one last spell. The journey has been long and tiresome. They're exhausted, and just want to rest. They lie down and fall into a deep sleep in a beautiful field. But they've strayed from the path, and are in danger of never waking up again.

Spiritual death threatens us in the same way, only without the flying monkeys. Our journey grinds us down. The attacks never stop, and the enemy is both powerful and clever. We play into the weaknesses of those around us and one day find ourselves thinking that maybe we need to stop going. Rest is important, but we need to find it in God, not in the comfortable environments we're blessed enough to find ourselves in. By getting off course and falling asleep, we risk never waking again, and consequently never reaching the ultimate destination we seek.

We have to finish. Jesus ("It is finished.") and Paul ("I have finished the race.") completed their work. To follow their example is to do the same. Here's the catch: The finish line is death.

Picture a champion sprinter striving for victory. That's how we're supposed to live: so eager to meet God that we race toward the end. Yet once again, that picture doesn't line up with what many of us are doing. Society is designed to run away from death. We've got surgical procedures, exercise facilities, and more to help us pretend we can stave off that finish line. If that doesn't work, we can always just lie down for the long nap in a field of denial.

On the road to Oz, the good witch Glinda appears like an angel and magically wakes up Dorothy and her companions. In the real world, divine strength is the force we need to carry us onward. Paul's words to the Ephesians are relevant to us today:

> Wake up from your sleep,
> Climb out of your coffins;
> Christ will show you the light!
> (Ephesians 5:14 *THE MESSAGE*)

It's that light that draws us away from death and into life. We don't have to slog through unknown valleys. The path has been cleared, not just by those who went before us but also by a God who refused to sit by and watch loved ones stumble into the darkness. God came to the land of the living dead so that the dead might live.

We don't have to pretend to be thrilled about the eventual end of our race. Just as a runner endures grueling strain to reach the end, we also must endure, sometimes with pain. But the finish line is only a momentary snapshot in time. The correct picture of eternity is seen on the faces of runners who complete the course: relief, elation, joy.

I once heard someone say that destiny is where you end up, and fate is how you get there. If that's true, we can't control our fate, but we can control our destiny. Death isn't optional, but we decide whether or not we'll live to the fullest for whatever time God gives us. In *The Shawshank Redemption*, a man named Andy Dufresne dreams of escaping from prison. After years of going nowhere he tells a friend that everything comes down a simple choice: You either get busy living or get busy dying. His decision leads to a new birth of freedom that inspires those around him.

As Abraham Lincoln said on that hill in Gettysburg, we have to dedicate ourselves with devotion to the great task before us. We are part of a great race. And like Lincoln, a bearded leader named Moses once stood to address his people (Deuteronomy 30). He was nearing the end of his life too. His finish line was in sight, but he had some parting words for the people to hear first. Moses' message from that day continues to confront us now. The past is irrelevant, he said. Life and death have both been set before you. The choice is yours. Choose life now.

ACKNOWLEDGMENTS

A lot of people made this book happen, and it's a bit strange to try to express my gratitude here in what feels like the way we used to sign yearbooks at the end of our freshman year. But here goes.

You get a lot of funny looks from people when they ask you what kind of book you're writing and you tell them that it's zombie nonfiction. Those looks get even stranger when you try to clarify by explaining that it's really about spiritual life but that there are also references to vampires, Muppets, and even a vampire Muppet.

A So I'm forever grateful for my friend, agent, neurosis manager, and hero, Amanda Luedeke. Not only did she *not* back away slowly after meeting me and hearing my ideas, she actually got excited. Put simply, Amanda, you rock. I appreciate everyone at MacGregor Literary.

All of the brilliant artwork in this book was created by Gary Morgan who worked on such a tight schedule he probably had to tape his eyelids open to stay awake. Awesome job, man.

I'm thankful for Lil Copan who also got excited about the possibilities of this project and even encouraged me to be my quirky, pop-culture-loving self.

Pamela Clements, Julie Backman, Hampton Ryan, Mary Johannes, Susan Cornell, and everybody at Abindgon all deserve major kudos. I'm also indebted to Andy Meisenheimer, who's kind of like the literary equivalent of Mr. Miyagi because he smiles and tells you to do hard things, and you want to call him names but then you listen and your book gets a lot better. A LOT better. Thanks to all of you for making this book so much more than I could have done alone. I'm so glad somebody gets me. So is my family. They were starting to worry.

Speaking of said family, I would be nowhere without Mom and Aunt, Bethany and Mark, and Shannon and Ryan. For anyone who thinks I'm bizarre, you should know that these people are partly to mostly responsible. Just one family dinner with us and you would understand. And to the youthful faces of Cain, Jake, Sam, Becca, and Tessa, your smiles and hugs always bring me back to life.

I've got some great friends as well. A lot of wonderful people have been supportive and rooted me on. A few have been especially helpful in making this book, and my life, better. Thank you Kim Wilson and Ellie Soderstrom—my earliest readers—for telling me which parts to kill and which to breathe new life into. I've been inspired by so many, especially the ultimate muse Leanne Shirtliffe and two pastors named Mike whose wisdom and love found its way onto these pages. Dave, you're my brother. Thanks for the encouragement and helping me research all those zombie and vampire movies. Karl, you're an amazing friend, willing even to get in the pit with me, and you inspire me more than you know. So many other names could fill up these pages. Be sure that I love you all.

Writers are nothing without readers, so thanks to you for taking some time to check out this book. To keep the yearbook theme going I'll just say that you're really cool, and I'm glad we got to know each other this year. I hope we sit next to each other in homeroom sometime.

Finally, to whomever created peanut-butter-and-jelly sandwiches, I am forever in your debt. I'm pretty sure they'll have those in heaven too.